# POWER UP

# POWER UP

## ESSENTIAL TOOLS *for* COMMITTED CANNABUSINESS LEADERS

**STEVE SCHEIER** *and*
**MICHAEL ASHLEY**

High Impact Press

*San Francisco*

2021

*Published by* High Impact Press

ISBN: 978-1-7378919-0-1

*Interior book design by* Claudine Mansour Design

First Edition

Printed in the United States of America

To those who've stretched my thinking
about power and leadership:

Diedra Barber
Charles M. Cooke Jr.
Steve Jobs
John Lewis
Niccolo Machiavelli
John Vasconcellos

To those brave, thoughtful, and
creative leaders in cannabis and hemp who are
doing all they can to serve humanity,
I hope this book inspires you to further greatness.

To Sarah, for infusing my life with
possibility, adventure, and love.

—Steve Scheier

To my wife, Valerie,
who shows me the power of love and support daily.

—Michael Ashley

# CONTENTS

# AUTHOR'S NOTE

There are two kinds of people: those who feel powerful and those who struggle with power. If you're someone who feels powerful (lucky you!) reading this book will provide you with leadership tools to cement your power.

But if you—like the great majority of people—struggle with power, use the tools in the following pages to enhance your thinking about power and how you can best wield it. Digging into power will enable you to grow more comfortable with this important life element.

The path to power is a lifelong endeavor you create as you go. There's no "freeway" to power. You build the road to power every day. Whether you feel powerful or find power awkward and disquieting, this book is your ally. If you follow its lessons, we feel certain you will emerge more powerful and armed to constructively use power to advance your cannabusiness and your life.

# FOREWORD

Over the centuries, many books have been written about how to achieve success and how to acquire power. But few authors have addressed the thornier topic of what to do *with* power once you have it and how by taking the right steps you can extend your relationship with power. Perhaps that's because power is so often associated with *abuse*. (We've all heard "power corrupts," and we fear to even contemplate power and its exercise might force us to face darker aspects of ourselves.)

For this reason, the mere *discussion* of power is often taboo in "polite" circles. But it need not be this way. Used properly, power *can* be a beautiful force for good. If you're a powerful person with good intentions, a good heart, and a good soul, if you're doing things for the right reasons, you can be an influence for good through the power you exercise. Even if your company is small, the ripple effects that you create can propagate throughout your community, benefiting all.

Speaking of collective good, this book is about power, specifically how entrepreneurs in the cannabis industry can use their newfound power to achieve personal success, build strong, responsible companies, and, most important of all, help others. Authors Steve Scheier and Michael Ashley have created an invaluable "How-To" manual for those who likely are tasting true power for the first time, are unaccustomed or even uncomfortable with wielding power, and who may even find the very idea of power to be anathema to their value system. The authors write in clear, everyday language, infusing each chapter with simple but impactful stories based on actual experiences. Their message about power is clear: "Use it or lose it." And, if you use it, use it well.

My personal interest in cannabis and power was sparked when my daughter, Sophie, then just eight-and-a-half months old, was diagnosed with a rare, low-grade brain tumor. Just days after this devastating news, I was put in touch with former TV talk show host Ricki Lake and her producing partner, Abby Epstein, who were preparing what became the Netflix documentary *Weed the People* (2018).

Through them, we learned of amazing clinical trials in which cannabis was being used to treat victims of pediatric cancer. A few weeks later, Sophie took her first dose of cannabis on camera. (Note: there was no psychoactive effect from the diminutive dose.)

Afterward, we witnessed miracle after miracle as the drug, combined with traditional chemotherapies, mitigated her seizures, accelerating her recovery from even major brain surgeries. We knew if our child could have success like this, there was potential for others to as well.

This experience led us to create the organization CannaKids to support further research and testing of cannabis in children suffering from cancer and other diseases. It also led me to co-found, along with Jeff Brophy, Dr. Anahid Jewett, and Tim Brahm, NKore Biotherapeutics, a company dedicated to saving lives through nontoxic therapies.

The fact is we had access to cannabis and the lifesaving benefits it delivered. But this would not have been possible without the combined efforts of hundreds, if not thousands, of people, who fought against an entrenched political and medical establishment that demonized this product for decades. (Previously, cannabis had been denied to the public by people with power. But it was also liberated by those people who found their own power to upend nearly a century of myth and prejudice.)

Of course, when my journey began, I didn't believe I had much power at all. My child was desperately ill. The medical establishment offered little encouragement. The one avenue offering hope was seemingly blocked by what looked like a solid wall of statutes, regulations, and demoralizing red tape.

However, due to a combination of focus, perseverance, and the support of like-minded mavericks, I began to enjoy minor victories. Each triumph only increased my power further until finally a breakthrough could occur. One thing I learned from this experience is that power ebbs and flows. But the more you can exercise your power, the greater your power becomes.

If you are in a leadership role, if you own or run a cannabis company, *you* have power. How is that power best employed? You can use it to benefit yourself: to make money, to buy more things. But a better use of your power is to also benefit others. Being a leader shouldn't just be about material acquisition. A powerful leader should also be a mentor. You should use your role to broaden and expand the minds of those you lead every day. You should also inspire them to believe they are capable of more than they believe they are.

At the same time, be aware of your own limitations. No one, not even top leaders at the world's top companies, knows everything. That is why business success is always a team effort. As a leader, you need to be constantly learning, constantly on the lookout for new ideas. For as Steve and Michael advise, acquiring knowledge will bring you more power.

That's why it's so beneficial to seek input from others. Create an environment in which people at every level of your organization feel safe about coming forward with new ideas about how goals can be reached. You never know where or from whom the next big idea will arise, increasing your power.

A word of caution is still required. Being a leader is *not* easy. You will find yourself in situations that make you uncomfortable. Likewise, a company will always face challenges. If, as an entrepreneur, you think you can develop a business plan and stick to it, you are mistaken. (When we make plans, that's when God starts laughing!) Therefore, you must be able to think on your feet, to solicit solutions from the best minds in your organization, and not view criticism, especially of the *constructive* variety, as a threat to your power.

You have worked hard to get to the position you are in today. Now, sit back, find a comfortable space, and get ready to absorb valuable lessons on leadership and power. The tips you will learn can not only help you be a more effective boss but can also make you more comfortable and happier with the power you have struggled so hard to attain.

—TRACY RYAN
*Los Angeles, California, 2021*

# INTRODUCTION

"Power needs a rebrand," so says Anna Wyatt, CEO of The Betty Project, an artisan-sustained cannabis microbusiness. Anna couldn't be more right. As of now, the idea of "power" is off-putting to many people. It's also anxiety-creating. Spooky. *Dangerous.*

And yet power *must* be properly harnessed if we ever hope to achieve our dreams and desires. Our hope is that reading this book on power will help you in three ways:

1. To think about power differently.

2. To get in touch with the power you possess.

3. To use your newfound power to grow your cannabis or hemp company and, by doing so, change the world.

What intrigues us about power is that such an essential concept is barely mentioned in our daily discourse. As Harvard Business School professor and author Rosabeth Moss Kanter once said, "Power is America's last dirty word. It is easier to talk about money—and much easier to talk about sex—than it is to talk about power. People who have it deny it; people who want it do not want to appear to hunger for it; and people who engage in its machinations do so secretly."

To Kanter's point, isn't it odd how something so crucial to our happiness, our development, *and our very existence*—is so seldom openly spoken of? One reason why we don't discuss power enough is perception. Power is seen as unseemly and uncouth. Except, of course, by those who have it. The truth is, those who fear power or aspire to have power *must* learn to acquire it and use it well.

This is what our book will teach you.

In the pages to come, we will offer instructive stories starring leaders in the cannabis and hemp industry. You will read both cautionary and aspirational tales exemplifying our *Power Up* principles. Armed with this knowledge, you can advance your leadership potential, making your organization and yourself more successful.

Taking the long view, it's evident we learn much about power from our family, friends, society, and culture. What we absorb at an early age impacts our thinking. Our views are also shaped by whether we view the world as unsafe or as a place of unlimited opportunity. As we grow up, we must come to grips with power, deciding what makes sense to us.

We all have our own "origin stories" related to power. As Jews one generation removed from the Holocaust, Steve's parents fell into the category of believing the world to be an unsafe place. Whether consciously or unconsciously, he picked up from them the idea it's better to exist in the shadows—lest harm come to you.

Through their actions and words, his parents communicated their views about power to him, influencing his thoughts and beliefs. As a shy kid, he tended to stay in the background, just like they instructed. Fearful of power, he spoke out only when necessary. Moving from Brooklyn, New York, to Redwood City, California, at age 12 didn't help his introversion. The intense culture shock caused him to be even more withdrawn.

Yet, after a couple of years acclimating to his new environment, he felt a bit more comfortable and had developed a few friendships. Steve wondered whether he could run for class president. Instead, Steve worked hard to get *his friend* elected. Why? First, Steve liked him. He also thought his support would strengthen their friendship.

But the real reason Steve stayed on the sidelines had to do with power. He was afraid to advocate for himself. Filled with self-doubt, he feared saying to the world, "Elect me!" Instead, the school administration appointed him "elections commissioner" to count the ballots of those who *did* advocate for power.

Upon being elected, Steve's friend turned on him. Mocking Steve's support, he turned on Steve in front of their mutual friends. "Some people are leaders," he told everybody. "Others are followers."

His words stung. Steve never forgot the humiliation he felt. But he had a point. Steve had chosen to be a follower. Even though his friend lacked maturity and grace in that moment, he was right.

Steve opted out of power. He was more comfortable in the background.

As Steve has gotten older and broadened his experience base, he's wrestled with power. *How much could he claim, and to what end?* Over time he's also watched and learned much from his dealings with powerful leaders, including the late Steve Jobs. Likewise, when he worked in the California State Legislature, he observed and reflected on how political leaders wielded power to advance their agendas.

Throughout his life Steve continued to seek out powerful people and, to the extent that he could, learn from them. When possible, he also guided them in what he believed to be the fair and thoughtful exercise of their power. Yes, Steve didn't often feel comfortable being number one, but he did his best to influence the decision-makers and power brokers he worked with.

After many years, Steve concluded *everyone* has the capacity for leadership and the right to claim personal power. Society might put you in or assume you to be in a follower role, but you don't have to stay there. It is not preordained who is a leader and who is a follower. You can use power and become a leader. And if you are in a leadership role, wielding power effectively, you too can become a better leader.

Informed by these insights, Steve and Michael offer the *Power Up* principles to cannabis and hemp operators so they can better understand power, establish a vision, develop their leadership, improve decision-making, and achieve their goals. After all, even if many of us feel too timid to say it, power is indispensable from true leadership.

Those cannabis and hemp operators wishing to flourish in a newly regulated environment can benefit from this point of differentiation. Too often, many of them think they can succeed based on just their product's genetic superiority or their strong brand position.

This is a fantasy. Yes, with federal legalization will come banking, more favorable tax treatment, interstate commerce, and financial investment. But that only means suddenly *everyone* will be able to stride onto this bigger playing field. Those operators willing to use the following insights on power, vision, leadership, and decision-making will gain a competitive advantage in an increasingly crowded marketplace.

Before delving in, one more point must be stated. It's all fine and well to take the "high road," thinking power is crass and those who talk about it or pursue it to be tactless bullies. But do so at your peril. Power wants to find a vessel. Either in you or someone else. Turning your back on power will not cause power to vanish.

Power is also not an option. Someone *will* get power—no matter what. The question is, do *you* want to be that person?

Ultimately, power is like any force of nature. Just like the elements: wind, earth, fire, and water, power is everywhere, and the opportunities to use it are endless. For all our reticence in discussing power, it is nonetheless built into who we are. As Steve's high school election experience showed, we can't hide from power—even if we try.

In this spirit, let us now rebrand power with this closing thought. Our ability to use power should be our "superpower." For we stand to make incredible progress in our lives once we dare to understand our power, using it to grow ourselves and those around us.

Power wants a vessel. It wants to be utilized. It does not want to be wasted. It *will* find people to harness it, those who can use it to make progress. Will it be you, or someone else? If you want to develop your power to move your cannabusiness forward, keep reading.

We hope you enjoy our thoughts and the challenge we offer. As Apple's ground-breaking advertising campaign once said: "Think Different." Yes, think different about power.

*Power Up.*

—STEVE SCHEIER *and* MICHAEL ASHLEY

# POWER UP

# PART I

# POWER

## *and*

# YOU

# Chapter

# YOU HAVE POWER, OWN IT

This is a book about power: where it comes from, who has it, how to get it, why it's important, how it should be used . . . and how it can be abused. But before we can dive into our discussion, we must define our terms. Just what *is* power?

Webster's dictionary defines "power" thusly: (1) the ability to act or produce an effect; (2) possession of control, authority, or influence over others.

In other words, power is about controlling or influencing yourself and others to *make things happen*. If you want to get things done—if you want to *succeed*—then you must understand and master the use of *power*. This might not seem like a very "evolved" perspective in the early 21st century, but as we will demonstrate repeatedly over the course of this book, the successful utilization of power is essential to reaching your goals.

Power is the foundation of all organizational improvement. Without a firm understanding of power, it's impossible to create a vision or improve leadership and streamline decision-making. Power is also the foundation upon which vision, leadership, and decision-making are built. A person with an unclear relationship with power is unlikely to succeed, and any organization they are leading will likely suffer.

To see this in action, we offer the following story. For years, a person we will call Malcolm and his four partners ran a cannabis company in the Bay Area. Poorly.

Though the quintet (as they liked to call themselves) began with the best of intentions, things were clearly falling apart. Over time, product quality had declined. Orders weren't shipping on time. Sales were heading south. Most concerning of all, customers were upset.

And they expressed their ire with their pocketbooks.

If the company's poor performance was ever a secret, it was now out among the staff. They knew the company was in trouble. The dire situation erupted in the angry tone of vendors. It also manifested in the way employee paychecks decreased as the company had to scale back. Demoralized and frustrated, workers were left to wonder when the next crisis would hit and if they could expect to keep their jobs.

Meanwhile, Malcolm and his partners had come to the increasingly obvious conclusion they needed a more direct and effective leadership approach. Too many things were falling between the cracks. Too much jockeying between the partners prevented true leadership. Someone had to step up and right this ship.

Before it was too late.

Yet even though they knew they were in trouble, none of the partners were willing to cede power to a single designated leader. The business may have been foundering, but they hesitated to give up the power they believed they had—even if it meant their ruination.

As one of the partners said to Steve in a moment of socially awkward candor, "I don't want to be anyone's slave." While he ultimately moderated his views, the underlying thinking was clear: "I'd rather fail than take orders." Not a helpful view. Their egos were seriously clouding their business judgment.

Of course, the five would rather not be in this situation at all. If they had it their way, they would just focus on growing and selling cannabis. Safely ensconced in their silos, they could hope and pray for the best. However, with bankruptcy looming, the partners came to accept the fact a major reconfiguration of power was needed, that one of them must be allowed to rise above his peers in their organization.

Over a series of months and meetings, the partners debated over who should take command. No easy answer presented itself. None of the five had anything close to senior leadership training. We're talking about five dudes who came together to grow and sell great flower and tinctures. They knew a lot about grow lights and sativa strains. But they didn't really know how to run a company. They just figured their passion for the plant would overcome any challenges. Of course, they were incorrect.

After many futile deliberations, one of the partners threw up his hands. "Okay. *Okay*. Someone has to step up and lead! Someone has to be the CEO. Who's it going to be?"

No one wanted the responsibility, so much so that

Malcolm noticed his partners backing their chairs away from the table. It was like a *Three Stooges* episode where each stooge retreats to make the other person the fall guy. It would be funny, except this was their livelihoods. *This was their baby*.

"I'll do it," Malcolm said at last.

The partners sighed in collective relief. But the problems had just begun. Would the other four really allow Malcolm to operate as a CEO, or would they question his every decision, undermining him at every opportunity? After all, the partners remained owners of the company, even though they ceded operational control.

Besides, Malcolm also couldn't help wondering:

- Would his partners actually support his leadership?

- Would the staff back him?

- Did he really feel confident enough to lead?

- Could he express his power in a positive way?

- Could he be a leader?

Malcolm was right to worry. His foray into the role of CEO *would* disrupt years of consensual decision-making. Not only that, but it would also throw off his dealings with a staff that had come to see him as one of their own, even though his technical title was "partner."

The most troubling aspect of all? Malcolm's inner critic plagued him. He honestly feared he didn't have the guts or insights to lead. These concerns literally kept Malcolm up at night. Tossing and turning, he struggled to silence the disturbing one-way dialogue: *You will be second-guessed. You will be criticized. You will be hated . . .*

As the sun came up the next morning, Malcolm's eyes remained glued to the ceiling. One thought ate at him. Those who were once his peers would now resent him in his role. Everything he loved about working at his company would disappear when he assumed his new title.

"What have I done?" he asked aloud.

●  ●  ●

When it comes to power, sometimes it can be given to you as it was for Malcolm. If and/or when you are suddenly thrust in a leadership role, here are several strategies to "take" power.

## DON'T ACT AS IF—ASSUME YOU ARE

When Steve met with Malcolm, he told him to keep his second guessing to a minimum. "Begin the journey. 'Assuming you are' means looking around to realize everyone is counting on you. It also means they will follow you *if* you make an effort to lead."

"But how?" Malcolm asked, tension rising in his voice.

"Well, for one, people must be convinced to follow. The person who steps up—in this case, you—doesn't have to be perfect."

"Good. 'Cause I'm not."

"But they must be willing to make an effort."

Malcolm shook his head. "I can't tell anyone else this, but honestly, I don't know what I'm doing."

"That's okay. Your team doesn't need to see the entire path. They just need someone to take the first step."

Unconvinced, Malcolm took a deep breath. "All right. Where do I start?"

Steve pointed to his head. "Here. How you enter into leadership will largely affect the course of your new role. You must assume you are that person in the position of power. Then move your team forward, step by step."

"That's it?"

"Not quite. Vigilance is required, Malcolm. It might sound easy now because I'm here supporting you, but you've got to *own* this thing. If you constantly doubt if you are 'that guy,' it will lead to your ruin."

## CREATE A VISION

People will follow you if you have a plan they believe can work. A vision is essential. Ask yourself:

- What do you stand for?

- What does your company stand for?

- What do you want to build?

These three questions must be answered before progress can be made. People who assume CEO roles without being able to answer these are doomed to fail. By the way, you can involve the whole team in this vision creation exercise, but *you* must drive it.

Create a vision so your team will take the leap.

## EXECUTE TO IMPRESS

After that conversation with Malcolm about his mindset, they moved on to tactics.

"Find a task that's been daunting the company, something that supports your mission and/or purpose, and accomplish it well," Steve advised.

"You mean, show them I'm in charge?"

"Almost, but not exactly. Being 'in charge' provides you with the opportunity to 'show the way.' But at its best, leadership is not about coercion. It's about vision and communication, reinforcing every day what it is you want to achieve, then doing it. Rather than trying to bombastically demonstrate that you possess power, *show* people via your actions how you can use power effectively and gain their respect."

Malcolm sat there in silence for a moment, thinking. Suddenly, he stood straight up. "Cultivation!"

"What about it?"

"One of my partners, Ed, is this wacky guy." Malcolm began pacing around the room. "He's self-taught, you know? But terrible at hitting milestones."

"I bet he's good at making excuses, though."

Malcolm frowned. "Because of him we can't hit our cultivation goal. That's why our revenue is way down. He's unfocused, and I need him to stay focused on the plants and their health."

"Yeah. If you can't grow it, you can't sell it."

Malcolm's frown deepened. "You know, Ed is one of the partners who put me in charge—he likes me. I like him. He's one of my biggest supporters."

I think I knew where he was going with this. His task wouldn't be easy.

Several days later, Malcolm called me. I noticed some of the tension in his voice was gone.

"I spoke with Ed about the cultivation challenges we face and his lack of focus. It was one of the first things I did in my new role."

"It was hard, right?"

"It sucked. But it had to be done. He wasn't happy with my assessment of his work. He blamed circumstances beyond his control. I think he resented my butting into his space. But after an hour of talking, he decided, with my encouragement, to leave the company. The new policies and procedures we need to implement to ensure our team gets it together were just more than he wanted to take on. It was for the best. And it's changed the whole way people look at me now. I acted rather than waiting out the situation. They're beginning to see me as a leader."

"And why do you think that is?"

Malcolm paused to think about his answer. "Because I was willing to do the hard shit for the sake of our company."

. . .

The lens through which you view the world is different when you become a leader. As a mere partner, Malcolm could tend to his own silo. He could focus on his own thing. He could even look past others' shortcomings.

After stepping up as CEO, he no longer had this luxury. This doesn't mean Malcolm is selfish or maniacal. It means he had to broaden his thinking.

The leader's worldview is different from someone on

the team. For leaders, *everything* and *everyone* matters. As a result, they must become discerning. They must suddenly worry about the whole rather than their part.

The good news is that, when placed into a leadership role, if you show your team what you are capable of—and get it right—people won't need to be *told* why they should follow you. They'll do it because they can see the results for themselves.

This is what happened to Malcolm. By taking a dramatic and important step, he earned his people's trust, which led to greater power. He did the hard work that was needed.

What Malcolm did might seem like an impossible task to you. But you don't have to be a superhero to run a successful cannabusiness. All humans come with power as standard equipment.

And yet people are often afraid to use their power. They worry what its usage might reveal about them. (Example: "It might mean others think I am bossy or bitchy.") Forget fading into the background. Forget being ashamed about your power. Step into your power and own it. As Legolas from *Lord of the Rings* told Aragorn, "Put aside the ranger. Become who you were born to be."

There's no need to fear power. You have it. Now advocate to be the one to show the way.

## POWER HOMEWORK

Get out a trusty notebook to reflect upon the following:

1. What are your feelings about power? How did they develop? Write down your thoughts. Dig

into your psyche a bit. How have your feelings about power helped *or* hurt you?

2. Take note of your power. Are you in a confusing power situation, or is your power in the organization relatively clear? If it's not, what must you do to make it clear?

3. Now, engage your team in a discussion on power. Share with them your thoughts and encourage them to do the same. Ask them if they feel powerful in their jobs. Tell them about your struggles with power and ask them about how they've struggled. Use this feedback to guide your own use of power.

*Chapter*

# NO, THEY'RE
# NOT YOUR FRIENDS

One reason many leaders fail to own their power is because they fear it will isolate them from others. They believe power divides people, and they're afraid of losing their social connections.

They have every reason to worry.

NBC's *The Office* (2005–2013), based on the British series created by Ricky Gervais, is a classic of American television. (Though not for everyone—Steve is not a fan! After reading this chapter, you may understand why.)

At the heart of the show is regional manager Michael Scott (Steve Carell), a mid-level, not-particularly-bright corporate suit whose desire to be both liked and respected borders on the desperate. In fact, Scott's obsessive yearning to be embraced as a loving father figure by his underlings is the source of much of the show's signature "cringe" comedy.

The more Scott struggles to be liked, the more pathetic he becomes.

Like any good comic idea, Michael Scott's character is rooted in bitter truth. There are thousands, if not *tens of thousands*, real-life "Michael Scotts" wreaking havoc in the cannabusiness world right now: men—and women—who think the way to run an office is to be "pals" with their staff.

You've come across many, no doubt. They try to engage direct reports in intimate personal conversations. They invite employees to after-hour activities or to their homes on weekends. They offer to do favors, provide personal advice, even lend money. The result is often as awkward and embarrassing as anything cooked up in a sitcom writer's room. The bottom line is, no matter how much we wish it wasn't the case, *leaders cannot be friends with their employees.*

This probably isn't what you want to hear. And because cannabis operators worked illegally for years, people had to trust and befriend the people they worked with and sold to. These early stage operators owed their liberty and safety to the relationships they forged. It can be wrenching to change and the legal market requires different behaviors. It's tempting to think those surrounding you at work are your buddies and their role is to support you. In the cannabusiness in particular, the last thing we want to create is the kind of cold, disciplined, corporate hierarchy so many of us view with disdain.

You can be "friendly" to your team, but you *can't* be their friend. It's just that simple.

As it turns out, hierarchy has some degree of virtue. In the end, *someone* must have a vision and put it into action. Hierarchy also creates organizational efficiency and productivity. Virtually every time someone thinks they can smash this standard business paradigm, chaos ensues.

Think about it: the oldest social structure in human history is the military. In existence since at least the Bronze

Age (3000 B.C.), the pyramid-shaped model with generals on top, officers in the middle, and "grunts" on the bottom, has remained nearly unchanged for five millennia.

No other social model even comes close. Why? Because it *works*. Especially in times of crisis. The person at the top has the vision and gives the orders. The people below understand them and may have to interpret them for the current situation, but ultimately, unless the orders are illegal or fundamentally stupid, they follow them.

It's how things get done, particularly when big, complex goals are at stake requiring the sustained actions of multiple people. But one thing militaries of every culture frown upon is *fraternization* between members of different ranks. Officers don't get chummy with enlisted troops. Senior officers don't even get close to junior officers. Such behavior leads to breakdowns in discipline and a loss of organizational effectiveness.

In the military, such weakness can lead to defeat—and death. Why? Because, as leaders, we must make choices, and these will be clouded if we get too close to those we lead. We must be mindful of everyone's humanity and even their goals while taking those steps necessary to advance the mission.

Of course, in the cannabusiness, we're not talking about conquering Mesopotamia or landing troops on the beaches of Normandy. We don't need to behave according to the rules of the Uniform Code of Military Justice. But the prohibitions against fraternization are similar—and serve a related purpose. To run a business, you often must take actions both uncomfortable and unpleasant.

For instance, you may have to choose one person for

promotion over a field of equally qualified candidates, thus disappointing and frustrating those you passed over. You may even have to sternly discipline an unruly employee, or worst of all, lay someone off.

But you're going to find it quite difficult to fire someone you lunch with every week. After all, can you really be objective about a manager's performance when you regularly confide in him/her about your fears? And how can you possibly discipline someone you've just played paintball with the previous weekend?

Then there's the issue of "optics." If you're friendlier with certain employees, others are likely to feel left out. They may accuse you of favoritism. (Even if they don't do so to your face.) Even if you make a special effort to be objective when it comes to salaries, promotions, and handing out assignments, having personal relationships can give the *appearance* of unfairness—and in a competitive professional environment, this can undermine employee morale and productivity.

It turns out, the old saying is true: *It's lonely at the top*. A boss must necessarily set himself/herself apart from everyone else. Here's another old, equally relevant adage: *If you want a friend in business, get a dog*. Your team is not there to support you. You're there to support *them*, and, by doing so, you will reach your goals.

Business and friendships don't mix from a power perspective. Leaders must get past their own emotional neediness. They must be okay with making hard, sometimes painful decisions that can upset others. When a leader is too concerned about hurt feelings or damaging friendships, they set themselves up for failure.

By the way, this isn't theoretical. We've seen many bosses fall into the friendship trap. It's all too common in the cannabusiness, where we naturally like to keep things loose and improvisational.

There was one CEO in particular who was really smart, really creative, really ambitious—but also really emotionally needy. Like Michael Scott, he wanted everyone to like him. He not only believed being liked was key to creating a smoothly running company, but he also feared being cast as the "villain" or the "exploiter" in his employee's minds.

To this end, he'd wander the office making casual conversation. Sometimes he would say to females, "You look pretty today." Or sometimes he would feel depressed and would ask, "Can I have a hug?" He'd invite workers to go outside and smoke with him. He'd tell employees personal secrets they had no business knowing. He'd even lend his employees money, destroying any semblance of clear boundaries.

This man clearly saw the culture of cannabis as something apart from "conventional" business. *I can trust these people as friends*, he thought. *My team is here to support me.* Yes, he wanted to be successful. He wanted the company to grow. And he wanted to make money. But his efforts to boost morale by forming personal bonds with workers had the opposite effect from what he intended.

People kept jockeying for his attention. This led to friction and bickering. Staff members began accusing him of playing favorites. Employees saw him as weak and blew off his suggestions and criticisms. There were also multiple complaints of unequal and unprofessional treatment.

As a result of this poor behavior, he lost his people's

trust. And as things began to (predictably) fall apart, he lost his temper with increasing frequency. He'd yell at people out of frustration. This only caused morale to sink further.

In the end, his company's board of directors decided he was not the leader the organization needed. Even though he had helped found the company, he was squeezed out.

So, what are the ground rules for effectively balancing power with emotional needs? Actually, they're quite simple:

1. Separate your work life from your personal one. You know the expression, *Don't shit where you eat?* Make it your mantra. Don't get involved with your employees. That goes for friendships and *doubly* so with romantic relationships. (That's material for a whole other chapter.)

2. Don't burden your workers with your problems. If your kids are sick or your mother has cancer or you've just discovered a slab leak under your house, don't tell your people this stuff. If these issues require you to be less available to your team, then give them a heads-up, but keep it to a minimum. Don't belabor it. They already have enough problems of their own to worry about.

3. You're still going to need friends and confidants, but find them *outside* of the office. Join a meet-up group. Attend a church, mosque, or synagogue of your choice. Maybe even talk to your neighbors. Just don't get chummy

with someone you may one day have to let go, discipline, or just guide. It doesn't work. Don't make life harder by thinking you can be "friends" with your people.

4. Being the boss doesn't mean you have to be aloof. You can still be cordial, pleasant, even sympathetic. In fact, many experts encourage leaders to be emotionally supportive. But that's the thing: you are there to support your team; they are not there to support *you*. Don't look to your direct reports for personal advice or emotional validation. Be friendly but not friends.

5. It's actually okay to take employees to lunch— as long as you're even-handed about it and keep the talk on a mostly professional level. Think of your role as that of a parent, not a sibling.

One of the pushbacks Steve regularly gets about avoiding friendships at work is that professional commitments can consume 8, 10, or even 14 hours a day, so where else *but* the office is one going to make friends? If this is your concern, your problem isn't finding friends, it's your work/life balance. Perhaps you need to step away from the job more often, delegate more, and make sure you have enough "Me Time."

Today, Steve has friends who used to work for him. But they became friends *after* they left the company. Since the leader/follower dynamic is no longer operative, they can treat each other as equals. Which is the way it should be.

With great power comes not only great responsibility, but also great sacrifice. But such is the nature of power. It must be wielded thoughtfully. It must be wielded wisely. And, to a great degree, it must be wielded coldly.

Because life is not a sitcom. And we are never guaranteed a happy ending.

## POWER HOMEWORK

Take stock of your situation. (Get out that journal we talked about at the end of chapter 1.)

1. Have you attempted to develop "friendships" on your team?

2. Have you burdened your team with your personal issues?

3. Do you favor your "friends" on your team to the detriment of others?

4. Do you consider your employee base to be part of your personal dating pool?

5. If the answers to any of the above questions are "yes," what difficulties have emerged from these practices?

6. If the answers to any of the above questions are "yes," what can you do to make amends and back away from these unhealthy relationships?

# Chapter

# BALANCE OF
# POWER REQUIRED

In the last chapter, we discussed how many leaders fear the isolation that comes with power. There is another major concern people have about assuming authority: that it will turn them into assholes.

Again, people have good reason to be concerned.

Once upon a time, the Roman Empire held sway over most of Western Europe. Its imperial armies reigned supreme over lands from the Iberian Peninsula in the west to Britannia in the north to Babylonia in the east to the entirety of North Africa in the south. During the Pax Romana, Rome's 200-year-old Golden Age, citizens and subjects enjoyed uncanny prosperity brought about by improvements in education, sanitation, irrigation, transportation, manufacturing, distribution, civil governance, and international trade.

Of course, we all know what happened after that.

Common wisdom holds that invading barbarians overwhelmed the self-satisfied Romans, leading to their downfall. Some historians disagree with this theory. Instead, they blame corrupt emperors for the empire's collapse. Infamous dictators like Caligula (37–41 C.E.), Nero (54–68 C.E.), Commodus (180–192 C.E.), and Maximinus Thrax (235–238 C.E.) wielded unquestioned power for personal profit or pleasure rather than for the good of their people. This led to internecine conflicts, civil war, and economic chaos, leaving the empire wide open for easy conquest.

Now let's jump ahead one-and-a-half millennia. In the mid-20th century, the Soviet Union was the dominant power in Eastern Europe. Possessing a brutally effective military on par with the U.S., the U.S.S.R. embarrassed the West with technological triumphs, including launching Sputnik, the first orbiting satellite, in October 1957, putting the first person in space in April 1961, and performing the first spacewalk in March 1965. Easily crushing democratic rebellions in Hungary, Czechoslovakia, and the Baltic states, the U.S.S.R. expanded its influence into Central America in the 1980s and appeared poised to remain a threat to the West well into the 21st century.

But two key events, both self-inflicted, weakened the Kremlin's power. The first was its ill-advised invasion of Afghanistan, an incursion that lasted years and severely crippled the Soviet economy. The other was the Chernobyl nuclear reactor meltdown in April 1986. In both cases, bureaucratic stubbornness and leadership's posture of infallibility made two bad situations infinitely worse. By the time nationalist rebellions erupted in Poland and other Eastern Bloc nations in the late 1980s, the Kremlin—now economically bankrupt and spiritually exhausted—simply had no power left to stop them.

These are just two examples illustrating a key challenge

of leadership. While leaders are installed to serve the interests of an organization, be it a company, a corporation, a nation, or even an empire, power has a natural tendency to focus its authority on little more than self-perpetuation. As Britain's Lord Acton so famously put it in the 19th century:

> Power tends to corrupt and absolute power corrupts absolutely. Great men are almost always bad men, even when they exercise influence and not authority; still more when you superadd the tendency of the certainty of corruption by authority.

Almost a century later, George Orwell, in his dystopian novel *1984*, had his own take on power's propensity toward self-perpetuation:

> Power is not a means; it is an end. One does not establish a dictatorship in order to safeguard a revolution; one makes the revolution in order to establish the dictatorship. The object of persecution is persecution. The object of torture is torture. The object of power is power.

What this means is that as you come into your own as a leader, as you obtain more and more influence, you must not allow the same ambition, confidence, and persuasion that once propelled you to the top overshadow your company's needs. You cannot allow yourself to fall into Lord Acton's trap: to let your moral authority be undercut by the power you now wield.

Or, as American lawyer and politician Robert G. Ingersoll reportedly said of President Abraham Lincoln: "Nearly all men can stand adversity. But if you want to test a man's character, give him power."

(Today, let's substitute "person" for "man" in the last sentence, but the point remains the same.) Fortunately, if you know in advance this propensity toward self-perpetuation exists, you can prepare yourself to do something about it. We call this state "Self-Aware Power."

As a leader, you must strike the right balance so that as you increase your power, it serves your wider organization and doesn't just benefit you. Why? If you do not put the brakes on power, it can be like a runaway train, taking *everyone* places they don't want to go.

When this happens, at first, no one will stop you. Instead, they'll rationalize your behavior, telling themselves it's your "right" to seize this power. Or they will say that "it's for the best." And if you're not stopped, you may come to feel you're invincible. But this is an illusion, and countless examples tell us if you try to seize too much power, you will be overthrown.

Power will always find a way to rebalance itself. History and business are replete with stories of people who have not possessed this balanced approach to power. They leave nothing but chaos and crisis in their wake. Some recent high-profile examples include:

- Harvey Weinstein, the high-powered, Academy Award–winning Hollywood producer (*The English Patient, Shakespeare in Love*) who used his influence to sexually exploit dozens of young actresses over decades. When his abuses were finally exposed during the #MeToo movement in 2017, he was forced to resign and was later found guilty of five felonies.

- Carlos Ghosn, who, having run an alliance of car makers, including Nissan, Mitsubishi Motors Corp., and Renault, was arrested by Japanese authorities in November 2018 for using a Dutch subsidiary to spend some $18 million buying and renovating personal homes.

- Former Tyco International chief executive Dennis Kozlowski, who squandered millions in unreported company money to finance a lavish lifestyle that famously included a $6,000 shower curtain.

- John Thain, former CEO of Merrill Lynch, who spent wildly on office décor even as his company lost $15 billion in Q4 2009. Among his infamous purchases were an $87,000 rug and a $1,400 trash can.

- Wayne LaPierre, CEO of the National Rifle Association (NRA), who, in 2019, was accused of spending almost $300,000 of his organization's money on his wardrobe, including a $39,000 suit.

Of course, not all such cautionary tales are so high-profile. Stories of small business owners and CEOs who got drunk on power are legion, even in the cannabis industry.

Steve knows of one cannabusiness CEO who, after being handed the keys to the kingdom, decided his position vested him with unlimited power but no personal responsibility.

As a result, he became the poster child for hypocrisy. He would demand his people work long hours, then habitually arrive late and leave early. He spent his evenings spending gobs of cash and partying with friends. One time he crashed his sports car spectacularly, causing injuries to his unlucky passenger. It was also an open secret he was sleeping with his assistant. He made no attempt to hide his excesses, and, as a result, his workers lost faith in him. Productivity cratered and he was ultimately shown the door.

Then again, it's possible to overcompensate—to tip the balance in the opposite direction, becoming so committed to your organization you neglect yourself. Back when Steve was working for Apple, he habitually burned the candle at both ends.

"Back then, I worked night and day. There was no shortage of calls. It seemed like everyone wanted my time and attention. And I liked it too. I was doing my small part to change the world. But things didn't turn out so well. My first marriage ended in divorce because I was not focused on my wife and family. I thought she would see how hard I was working, how much money we were making, and be thrilled. But that was the attitude of a thirty-year-old desperate to succeed, hoping, *believing* the long hours I put in would make that a reality. Instead, it was exhausting, leading to tunnel vision, and wrecking the life I wanted," he said.

Of course, one of the reasons cannabusiness leaders go into this industry in the first place is they want to work in a venture where they can control their own destinies or at least have the illusion of doing so. (To re-quote the leader cited in our first chapter, "I don't want to be anyone's slave.")

As insensitive as his remarks might seem, he wasn't trying to be a jerk. He was just exuding a need for autonomy. He did not want to answer to others. He wanted the power to act as he saw fit. But unfettered power can destroy organizations and the people in them.

As a leader in the cannabusiness, you must practice "Self-Aware Power." Think of Self-Aware Power as controlled power. Your power should be like that emanating from a nuclear reactor. If there's too much or too little power flowing from the reactor, you'll get a Chernobyl-style event. The power with the longest-lasting influence flows smoothly with few fluctuations. You know when you're out of control or acting sluggish. This means you're not functioning from a position of sustainable and true power. If you stay mindful of this insight, your conscience will guide you toward the most efficient use of your power. Self-Aware Power can also help you rein in excesses, so you don't wield it irresponsibly or harmfully.

Be sure you don't deplete yourself or your company. Remember, powerful leadership is a long game. You must sustain yourself in all manners for the marathon.

## POWER HOMEWORK

Please take out your journal to reflect on how often you operate within and outside of the "Self-Aware Power Zone."

1. Do you vacillate between low power and run-away power, or are you consistent?

2. When and if you're demonstrating low power, why does this occur and what happens?

3. If and when you're demonstrating runaway power, why does this occur and what happens?

4. How often are you in the "Self-Aware Power Zone," feeling truly in control and powerful?

5. If you see yourself as vacillating between the poles of power, discuss this with a trusted colleague, entrusting this person with the responsibility of providing you feedback on your use of power.

# Chapter

4

# POWER CHANGES— FOREVER AND ALWAYS

People tend to think of power as a prize. Once we have acquired it, it's ours to keep. Forever.

Of course, nothing could be further from the truth.

We have all heard Aesop's fable of "The Tortoise and the Hare." In the story, the Hare, famous for his speed, mocks the Tortoise for his lumbering pace.

"How do you ever get anywhere?" the Hare chides the Tortoise.

"Oh, I manage," the Tortoise replies. "In fact, I bet I can beat you in a race."

Stunned by the Tortoise's ridiculous challenge, the Hare agrees to the contest. After all, how can he possibly lose? The day of the Big Race comes. At the referee's signal, the two competitors take off. The Hare—being, well, a hare —shoots off like a rocket.

Within minutes, he's left the Tortoise in the dust. "This is ridiculous," the Hare snorts, barely out of breath. "It's such a beautiful day. Why am I even wasting my time with this guy?"

Figuring the race is already in the bag, the Hare decides to enjoy the sunny afternoon. Settling into the grass beside the road, he soon drifts off to sleep. Hours pass. Meanwhile, slowly but steadily, the Tortoise makes his way down the road, passing the sleeping Hare. Still, the Hare sleeps on. More hours pass.

Finally, a cool evening breeze awakens the Hare from his slumber. Peering around, he sees no sign of his challenger. Convinced he's still far ahead, he takes off at a leisurely pace toward the finish line. Only when he has crested the last hill does reality sink in: the Tortoise is just about to cross the finish line! His heart pounding, the Hare switches to warp speed, but it's too late. The Tortoise crosses comfortably ahead of the Hare.

It's an ignominious defeat the Hare never lives down.

The moral of this tale is usually said to be: "Slow but steady wins the race" or "The race is not always to the swiftest." But there is another lesson to be gleaned. It's a cautionary tale about the arrogance of power. People who find themselves blessed with advantages too often believe their positions are unassailable, that once they have achieved a degree of success they can—like the doomed Hare—just coast through the rest of their lives.

In fact, nothing is further from the truth. Power is *always* being challenged. And it must always be defended against a myriad of challengers. Get out of the "Status Quo Is Okay" mentality. Instead, expand your thinking. Be fluid. Grow with the times. Otherwise, the times will outgrow you, devastating you and your organization.

So, what's the surest way to lose power? Through complacency. The landscape of American business is littered with the bones of companies and CEOs who believed their leadership positions were untouchable, only to learn the price of hubris. For example:

- Kodak was once the undisputed leader in photographic film manufacturing and processing. In 1975, a company engineer named Steve Sasson invented a digital camera he promoted to leadership as the future of photography. But Kodak's chiefs believed nothing could replace good old-fashioned film—the technology upon which the company built its fortune. They politely passed on Sasson's invention. Now jump ahead 30 years. In January 2012, having been totally eclipsed by digital camera manufacturers, Kodak had to declare Chapter 11 bankruptcy.

- In the 1980s and 1990s, Blockbuster was the king of the video rental business. Around the turn of the millennium, it operated more than 9,000 brick-and-mortar stores throughout North America. Early in 2000, it had a chance to buy a young upstart called Netflix for $50 million. Seeing little profit in Netflix's home delivery service or its off-the-wall "streaming" proposals, it passed on the offer. Ten years later, Blockbuster was out of business. Today, Netflix is valued at almost $200 billion, making it more valuable than Disney.

● For decades, Barnes & Noble was synonymous
with books. Their massive retail stores domi-
nated shopping malls from coast to coast. In the
mid-1990s, young Jeff Bezos challenged Barnes
& Noble's retail supremacy by offering a wide
range of books online at deep discounts. The
reaction of Barnes & Noble's leadership was
one of bemusement. After all, Barnes & Noble
didn't just offer books. It offered *experiences*.
When people buy books, they like to browse,
right? They like to sit down and have some coffee. Management had to eat their words. Today,
Barnes & Noble is just a shell of its former self.
And Jeff Bezos's little company? Amazon.com
is the largest retailer in the world, selling everything from books to electronics to groceries.
Meanwhile, Bezos himself is one of the richest
men on the globe with an estimate net worth of
more than $200 billion.

● ● ●

So, once you obtain a modicum of power, how do you
protect it from would-be competitors? Absolute rulers
throughout history often preserved theirs by simply elim-
inating their competition. Kings, emperors, and dictators
dealt with usurpers through violent means including arrest,
imprisonment, torture, and execution.

Today, leaders of criminal organizations, like drug
cartels, remain fond of this direct approach, "whacking"
threats that become too pronounced. Of course, those of
us who operate in the legitimate business sphere must be

more circumspect than a Pol Pot, Josef Stalin, or Pablo Escobar. We must retain our power by actually *deserving* it.

One of the most effective things you can do to hold on to power is *keep learning*. Knowledge *is* power, and the more you know, the more people will look to you for guidance. Not only has continuing education always been a proven key to long-term success, but the world is changing so fast you risk being left in the dust if you don't keep up on the latest advancements.

To this end, make it part of your daily routine to read newspapers, either online or in old-fashioned print, as well as industry-relevant websites, books, and trade journals. And don't just confine yourself to news about the cannabusiness. Events in the broader world of local, national, and global politics, agriculture, law enforcement, health, medicine, manufacturing, finance, retailing, and transportation can have a big impact on your company now and in the future.

It's also helpful to watch videos, especially TED Talks and similar educational presentations, to broaden your mind and grow your understanding of the world and your place in it. Likewise, attend industry conventions and trade shows to see where the cannabusiness is heading. You can learn from peers, too, gaining intelligence on your competition. After all, the more you can project to your team that you have your finger on the pulse of the industry, the more trustworthy you will seem.

Along the same lines, it behooves you to never stop looking for flaws and cracks in all areas of your operations. Be forever on the lookout for ways to do better, because as we have said, you as the leader bear the ultimate responsibility for your company's success. Knowing what is true—or what's working today—may have no relevance tomorrow. You must constantly keep your eye on the ball.

Above all, develop your sense of self-awareness. Understand that despite your success and lofty station, you are flawed like every other human. Recognize you are not infallible, and that hubris and complacency inevitably lead to ruin. (Just ask the Hare!)

Case in point: a cannabis CEO named Frank once created an impressive growing operation in eastern Washington. He felt strongly about his product, insisting it be grown organically. He nurtured his plants like a father doting on a child. But Frank suffered from a serious debilitation he refused to recognize. He acted like a sociopath.

Now, contrary to how they are depicted in Hollywood fiction, sociopaths are not all mass murderers. ("Sociopathy" is simply a heightened level of narcissism and extreme self-involvement that makes it difficult for an individual to relate to others or experience empathy.)

For the most part, sociopaths have a conscience—unlike psychopaths, who do not—but it's weak. Although they can usually distinguish between right and wrong, their desire—their *need*—to always be right usually supersedes moral considerations.

In Frank's case, his sociopathy manifested in worker abuse. He demanded total fealty from his people. He made them work long hours but paid them below market rates. He responded to even minor errors with rage and insults. And once, to get his people's attention, he fired a pistol into the air.

Oh, it gets worse.

Another time, when frustrated employees (justifiably) confronted Frank about their owed back wages, he pulled a wad of cash from his pocket, threw it on the ground, then pissed on it.

"There's your money," he snarled.

Not surprisingly, his workers responded the way impoverished French peasants did to the reign of Louis XVI. They revolted. No, they didn't drag Frank to the guillotine. But they did secretly sabotage his crops. They badmouthed him to suppliers. They stole equipment from his greenhouses. And many simply upped and quit.

Had Frank understood himself better, perhaps he could have learned to curb his worst impulses. Instead, he let power go to his head—and paid the price. Bottom line: just because you have power at one moment doesn't mean it's eternal. If you mistreat people, they will find ways to reclaim it. Power will always rebalance.

## POWER HOMEWORK

Again, take out your journal and think about the following:

1. Have you been in situations where you lost power?

2. What actions caused this loss?

3. What lessons did this experience reinforce in you?

4. What steps have you sometimes taken to make "sure" power stays with you?

**5.** What have been the costs and benefits of these approaches?

**6.** Do you labor under the belief you will always be powerful?

**7.** What will happen to you if you lose power?

# PART 2

# POWER

*and*

# TRUST

# Chapter

# THERE ARE NO SMALL BREACHES OF TRUST

For any relationship to endure, trust must exist between the participants. This is true in marriage. This is true in friendship. And it is true in business. A company in which the leaders don't trust the employees and/or the employees don't trust the leaders is doomed to fail.

But trust is not something you demand. Like power itself, trust is something you *earn*.

In his best-selling book, *Sapiens: A Brief History of Humankind,* Israeli historian Yuval Noah Harari notes how humans came to dominate the planet for one simple reason: our capacity to work cooperatively in large groups— even as strangers. Cities are built, economies are created, wars are fought, and empires are established by people who share beliefs, values, and goals rooted in little more than mutual trust.

According to Harari, this means when you pass a stranger on a busy city sidewalk, you can trust they're not going to knife you. Likewise, when you buy groceries at the market, you can trust the fruit isn't tainted and the box labeled "Frozen Pizza" really has a frozen pizza in it. When you go to work for a company, you can also trust you'll be paid the agreed-upon wage and your managers will behave in an ethical manner. Likewise, as a boss, when hiring employees, you can trust they will perform the tasks for which they have been retained and will do so with diligence and professionalism.

Of course, sometimes, trust *is* breached. Sometimes the stranger you pass on the street really *is* a homicidal maniac. Sometimes the fruit you buy at the supermarket *is* laced with dangerous pesticides. Sometimes executives turn out to be jerks, sociopaths, or even outright crooks, and sometimes employees turn out to be slackers, embezzlers, petty thieves, or industrial spies.

When this happens—once the social contract of trust is violated—things start to fall apart. Fast.

How many marriages ended in divorce because one partner cheated on the other? How many politicians have been voted out of office or forced to resign in disgrace when they took actions that "violated the public trust"? How many companies have gone belly up when the public caught wind of their improprieties, malfeasance, or outright fraud?

Over the years, sages have had much to say about trust. And they all note it's a powerful but fragile concept:

> "Trust takes years to build, seconds to break, and forever to repair."
>
> —*Dhar Mann*

"Would you want to do business with someone who was 99% honest?"

—*Sidney Madwed*

"Trust but verify."

—*Ronald Reagan*

Yet as fragile as trust is, most pundits agree with Harari that trust is the stuff that binds civilization together:

"You must trust and believe in people or life becomes impossible."

—*Anton Chekhov*

"Trust is the glue of life. It's the most essential ingredient in effective communication. It's the foundational principle that holds all relationships."

—*Stephen Covey*

"One must be fond of people and trust them if one is not to make a mess of life."

—*E. M. Forster*

Okay, so where does trust come from? And how is it lost? Trust comes from consistency. From the keeping of promises. From fulfilling commitments—no matter the cost. It comes from honesty.

In business, the words "trust" and "brand" are synonymous. Any experienced marketing expert will tell you a "brand" is a business's most crucial asset. Contrary to popular belief, a "brand" is not a name. It's not a logo. It's not a slogan. (Although all of these can represent a "brand.") No, a brand is a *promise* made to the public. The more consistently that promise is kept, the more the public comes to trust a company, thus the more the brand is worth.

Consider McDonald's, one of the most valuable brands in the restaurant industry. Why is its brand worth billions? Is it because the company produces outstanding hamburgers? Because their breakfast menu is worthy of a Michelin star? Hardly. No, the McDonald's brand is valuable because the company has made an explicit/implicit promise to its customers: that it will deliver "value-priced" fast food of consistent flavor and quality in a clean, family-friendly setting. (And this promise holds true regardless of where that McDonald's happens to be: Detroit, Michigan; Beverly Hills, California; or Shanghai, China.)

Clearly, the company works hard to maintain its promise, which has been key to its decades of success. Likewise, Disney built a world-class brand by promising high-quality, family-friendly entertainment, whether in the form of movies, TV series, theme parks, merchandise, or publishing. In the 1980s, when the newly revitalized company tried to branch out into more "adult"-themed entertainment, including its first R-rated films, it spent millions establishing two new film divisions, Touchstone Films and Hollywood Pictures, so as not to violate the promise of its family-friendly Disney brand.

Unfortunately, economic pressures and greed sometimes cause decision-makers to renege on promises they made to the public. Faced with hard choices, they opt to cut corners. They compromise on quality. They sacrifice consistency. They find maintaining high standards is expensive—and exhausting. (Because it usually is.) And thus, they lose their customers' trust. They undercut the value of their brand. *And they lose their power.* Jeff Doiron, chief revenue officer of PHX Technologies, summed it up perfectly when he told Steve, "People in cannabis often want to skip steps. They have weed, they see a market and think they'll be millionaires overnight. But it takes time and significant effort to build any company, particularly a cannabis company. There are no shortcuts. Do the work."

Building a brand also takes time. And effort. For millennia, the public has been taught to be wary of anyone trying to sell them something. The old Latin phrase, *caveat emptor*—"Buyer Beware"—no doubt has its roots in consumer paranoia going back to the Stone Age. As the leader of a cannabusiness, you must therefore do everything you can to build consumer and employee trust and keep it. For if you breach it, even in small ways, it will cripple your reputation, perhaps permanently.

Don't believe us? Remember Arthur Andersen & Co.? For decades, it was considered one of the top accounting firms. Its clients included the Federal Home Loan Mortgage Corporation (Freddie Mac), Merck & Co., Delta Airlines, and Costco. Its eponymous founder, who died in 1947, was a stickler for honesty and helped establish the then-nascent profession's standard of ethics.

But, in 2002, Andersen was revealed to have "cooked the books" for Enron, the notorious Houston-based energy company, resulting in one of the biggest bankruptcies in American history. With the company's reputation in tatters, its clients abandoned it, leading to the firm's swift and percussive collapse.

Lehman Brothers is another example of what happens to even seemingly bullet-proof companies that breach the public trust. Founded in 1850, the banking giant was a Wall Street exemplar until February 2007 when the public learned it had aggressively—some would say, *recklessly*—invested in the inflated subprime mortgage market. When those mortgages defaulted in early 2007, Lehmann did everything it could to cover up its poor decisions, but it was too late. It filed for Chapter 11 bankruptcy in September 2008, helping to trigger the financial collapse now known as the Great Recession.

Now, your cannabusiness may not (yet) have the stature or influence of an Enron, Arthur Andersen, or Lehman Brothers. But that doesn't mean your actions can't have major repercussions within your sphere. In fact, as an executive, any breach of trust you make can have an *exponentially* negative effect when compared to an employee breach. Theirs will produce a one-to-one effect. Yours can be a 1,000-to-one!

After all, responsibility for your company's behavior starts and ends with *you*.

Then again, the need to build trust extends not only to your customers and suppliers, but to your employees as well. Employees who trust their leaders tend to be more efficient, more productive, and, best of all, more profitable. On the other hand, when employees *don't* trust their leaders, work slows, quality faulters, defections increase, and profits tumble.

As it does with customers, building trust with employees

begins with *honesty* and *consistency*. You must keep your promises, whether they pertain to job responsibilities, office hours, employee compensation, fringe benefits, career investments, worker safety, or other considerations.

Break any of your promises and *you* will be the one paying the price.

This discussion begs two questions. Why do leaders feel they can renege on their commitments? And why do they think they can get away with whatever they want? Simple: they have an ill-informed/undeveloped view of power. They think, "I have power, so I can do what I want." They don't realize power ebbs and flows and they are merely its custodian, *not* its source.

As a leader, you must either commit yourself to performing at the highest level of trust, or you shouldn't bother running your business at all. It can be helpful to imagine there's a power barometer next to your head every day. You're either gaining or losing in the game of power. To get/keep it, you desperately need to keep this number up.

Think you can be excused for being "super busy" or because you're "under pressure"? Nope. That just won't cut it. Customers and employees don't care for excuses. All they care about are *results*. And if those outcomes don't match the expectations you have set, you're toast. (You wouldn't accept a breach of trust from your employees, and they won't accept one from you.)

To this point, a woman we will call Amanda once ran her company like a tyrant. She demanded perfection and fealty from her employees, but loyalty ran only one way. If she missed a deadline, she blamed her underlings. She would routinely yell at staff during meetings, publicly humiliating them. She once hired a recent college graduate to be her "second in command," but then changed her mind, relegating her to working in the stock room.

Due to her bad and inconsistent behavior, fear seized her business's culture. Employees dared not speak up for fear of reprisal. Because she routinely overpromised and underdelivered, customers also abandoned her for the competition. One of those rival businesses recognized what was happening and began poaching Amanda's talent, promising them respect and opportunity as well as a paycheck. Even when she lost a half-dozen key people, Amanda still saw only selfishness and disloyalty among the departees when she should have been looking in a mirror.

You can avoid this fate by creating a commitment list. Document all the promises you have made to your staff, your customers, and your suppliers. Review this list daily and hold yourself accountable for delivering on your promises.

Because people don't trust words. They trust actions. And your team is always watching you.

## POWER HOMEWORK

Using your journal, let's take stock of your situation.

1. Have you breached trust with anyone in your organization?

2. Are you seen as someone who keeps their word and doesn't make excuses? Or are you in the opposite camp?

3. When you've broken trust with someone in your organization or failed to deliver on your own goals, what do you tell yourself to justify this action? Do you make excuses, or are you honest with yourself and the person whose trust you broke?

4. Get some feedback. Ask members of your team whether you're perceived to be a keeper of your word or someone who blows with the wind?

5. If the feedback you receive from others makes you realize the level of trust others hold of you is not high, ask members of your team what you can do to rebuild your trust level. Listen to this feedback, then act on it.

# *Chapter*

# POWER DOESN'T COME FROM A TITLE

Even though you have a title and the power accompanying it, you still must earn the trust of your people so they will recognize your leadership. A title alone does not bestow trust.

Consider the power that comes with royalty, by definition, a hereditary power system. Kings pass their power down to their heirs, traditionally their firstborn sons. No special skills, training, or education are needed to assume magisterial authority, merely the luck of being born to the right parents in the right place at the right time. Yet, by convention and tradition, subjects ranging from the lowliest peasants to the highest-ranking nobles are expected to obey and defer to whoever sits on the throne.

Because kings (and queens) need not earn their position but must merely possess the proper genetics of an opportune birth order, the history of royalty is rife with monarchs who were painfully piss-poor potentates, including:

## ● CALIGULA (12–41 A.D.)

The mad Roman emperor's reign has become synonymous with terror, debauchery, corruption, and degeneracy. Fond of lavish living, combined with murder and incest, he was ultimately assassinated at the ripe old age of 28.

## ● RAMAGUPTA (4<sup>TH</sup> CENTURY A.D.)

The hereditary ruler of northern India's Gupta Empire, Ramagupta gained infamy when, after botching an attack on his arch enemies, the Saka, he agreed to a ransom requiring him to surrender his wife, Dhruvadevi, to the enemy king. Neither the woman nor Ramagupta's family was happy with this arrangement, so Ramagupta's brother threw the hapless monarch off the throne, defeated the Saka, then married Dhruvadevi himself.

## ● KING JOHN (1199–1216 A.D.)

The usurper brother of Richard the Lionheart memorialized in *The Adventures of Robin Hood*, King John was a real-life ruler whose incompetence was so extreme he was forced to sign the Magna Carta just to prevent a brewing rebellion by the English nobility. That didn't stop him from then launching a disastrous war with France, sealing his reputation as a royal nincompoop.

## ● CZAR PETER III (1728–1762 A.D.)

Grandson of the legendary Peter the Great, Peter III was born in German Prussia, hated

Russia, and only became czar because his older brother, Peter II, had the temerity to die of smallpox at age 14. Having no real interest in running a continent-spanning empire, he was deposed by troops loyal to his far savvier wife, who assumed the title Catherine the Great—and then had Peter assassinated.

### ◉ KAISER WILHELM I (1797–1888)

Although he dreamed of greatness, Kaiser Wilhelm was a weak, ineffectual man who delegated virtually every decision to his far more capable prime minister, Otto von Bismarck. Wilhelm I's only meaningful legacy was Wilhelm II, the man who launched the first World War, while Bismarck became known as Europe's greatest politician, lending his name to a legendary battleship, an incredible pastry, and the capital of North Dakota.

These examples of miserable monarchs prove a simple point: a great title does not make one a great leader. A title may bestow authority, but it does not instantly grant one competence, courage, vision, charisma, patience, intelligence, empathy, resilience, curiosity, or any of the other attributes we usually associate with leadership.

In short: titles don't mean shit.

Not that we don't love them. Many people who found cannabusinesses are fond of brandishing monikers like "CEO" and "President" as if the title alone makes one worthy of respect and adoration. By being the "big boss," they believe others should sit up, take notice, and accept their word as gospel. Some even think being "Top Dog" grants them a degree of omniscience and invulnerability, that they suddenly know all and can do no wrong. They demand fealty. Loyalty. Deference. Any criticism or push-back is regarded as high treason.

But claiming a lofty title is but the first step in becoming a true leader. Once you have power—and the responsibility that comes with it—you must demonstrate to your team you honor that power and will do what it takes to be an effective and consequential leader. (This is made doubly difficult by the fact we've all had bosses who were arrogant, tyrannical assholes whose lack of self-awareness left us skeptical of anyone so presumptuous as to fancy themselves a leader.) Worse yet are those executives put in positions of power because of familial connections, i.e., siblings, children, in-laws, etc. who then wield authority like the inbred Hapsburgs.

You want respect? You want loyalty? You want trust? Then you'll have to earn it.

So, what does *earning* power entail? It means walking the talk. Daily. It means facing problems head-on. It means creating big visions, then following through. It means keeping promises. Taking responsibility. Recognizing and awarding achievement. Helping others succeed. It means doing the right thing—especially when no one is watching.

Steve has met people with lofty titles who clearly were not up to the task. One was a guy we'll call Larry. Excuse me. *Dr.* Larry. Dr. Larry had received a Ph.D. in botany from a prestigious university and insisted on being called "Doctor" whenever addressed. He wore his doctorate like a badge of honor. Or rather, in the manner of an Old West sheriff, as a badge of authority. He believed his degree made him an expert in virtually *everything*, and openly demeaned anyone he believed had an inferior education.

But a Ph.D. in botany does not necessarily qualify someone to run a growing company (even if that company is involved with, well, *growing*), as Dr. Larry soon discovered. Although he was named CEO of a cannabusiness, he quickly found himself over his head, and all his arrogance and bluster couldn't turn his bottom line black.

But Dr. Larry was too insecure to ask for help. He was also too self-absorbed to imagine others might know more than he did. Clinging to his doctorate like a life preserver, he belittled everyone in sight, blaming *them*, not himself, for his company's failures. Ultimately, his investors had enough and replaced him.

Apparently, Larry was *not* what the doctor ordered.

Another cannabusiness owner had a somewhat different problem. Let's call him John. Because his was a privately held company, John had no board of directors to answer to. Which meant John was the supreme authority. And he definitely saw himself as such. But much like Germany's Wilhelm I, John preferred to delegate authority rather than wield it himself.

In fact, John was so committed to delegation he would disappear for weeks at a time, leaving his employees to run the business themselves. Where was John? On his boat.

John loved to sail. His dream was to journey around the world. So he'd practice. First by racing from Los Angeles to Ensenada, Mexico. Then he would spend four weeks on a crew racing from Los Angeles to Honolulu. But, unlike Wilhelm, John had no Otto von Bismarck to keep his business afloat. Leaderless—and rudderless—all John's good employees started looking for work elsewhere. Like a boat with multiple leaks, the cannabusiness began foundering until it capsized, leaving John with nothing but his title.

On the flip side, consider a cannabusiness CEO we'll call Mike. He was a whiz at business but not what you would call a "people person." Although he had a mind like a quantum computer, he had the inspirational powers of a cinderblock.

Fortunately, he also had what so many Top Dogs lack: self-awareness. He possessed a strong but not overwhelming ego. Determined to see his company succeed, he hired a more traditional "leader" to serve as CEO while he demoted himself to chief financial officer, a role he was far more comfortable playing. And, as a result, his company flourished.

So, here's the bottom line: don't let power go to your head. A title may give you authority, but it does not grant you trust, and it certainly doesn't bestow wisdom. These are things you must work for.

We will close this chapter by quoting the final monologue from the 1970 Academy Award–winning movie, *Patton*, written by Francis Ford Coppola and Edmund H. North on the subject of the temporary nature of power:

"For over a thousand years, Roman conquerors returning from the wars enjoyed the honor of triumph, a tumultuous parade. In the procession came trumpeters, musicians, and strange animals from conquered territories, together with carts laden with treasure and captured armaments.

The conquerors rode in a triumphal chariot, the dazed prisoners walking in chains before him. Sometimes his children, robed in white, stood with him in the chariot or rode the trace horses. A slave stood behind the conqueror holding a golden crown and whispering in his ear a warning: that all glory is fleeting."

## POWER HOMEWORK

Reflect on the following in your journal:

1. Have you abused and pushed people around with your title?

2. Do you use your title to push your ideas—even when you know they're suspect?

3. Have you taken a title for yourself while denying the same consideration to other members of your team?

# Chapter

# GROW YOUR POWER PEOPLE

In the past few chapters, we have talked a lot about trust. In addition to honesty and consistency, another powerful way to earn trust is to allow your people to grow as leaders. Subordinates who are unable to grow will, sooner or later, leave.

But this raises a key question: How do you prepare your people to assume the authority with which you will entrust them? And, once you have given these people power, how do you keep them from using it for their own purposes or, worse yet, turning it against you?

Daunting questions, right? They can feed into many powerful businesspeople's paranoia, affecting how much they delegate, if at all. In response to their (sometimes well-founded) fears, they guard power jealously, worried their subordinates will fail to use it properly, abuse it, or try to consolidate it for nefarious purposes. They even keep potential heirs away from the levers of power out of concern it will be turned against them.

Failing to groom subordinates to wield power may seem

like a clever move, as it makes you appear indispensable. (*Game of Thrones*, anyone?) But, in more instances than not, its effect is just the opposite. It actually undermines your company's stability, its capacity to weather adversity, and, most serious of all, its ability to function without you.

If you're breaking your back to start and grow a cannabusiness, you're probably doing so to support a comfortable lifestyle for yourself and your family. You may want to someday sell the business, pocket your riches, and fly off to a tropical paradise to savor your Golden Years. Or your ambition may be to one day pass the business along to one of your children. You may even dream of a cannabusiness legacy continuing for decades—or centuries—after you have shuffled off this mortal coil.

Whatever your ambitions, realize none of it will be possible if you *and you alone* know how to run your company. Realistically, no matter how well you manage your health, there will be times when you're unable to work due to illness, injury, emergencies, or other pressing demands.

What's more, no matter how much you love your work, there may come a time—hell, probably *many* times—when you just want to get away. And since none of us are immortal, there is always the possibility you will die, perhaps suddenly and unexpectedly. (Again, *Game of Thrones*, anyone?) In any of these situations, your company might suffer irreparable harm if you haven't selected people to assume power and haven't trained them to step into your shoes.

Once more, let's turn to history for illustrative examples of great companies that foundered when their founder was no longer in charge:

● Walt Disney was one of the 20th century's greatest entrepreneurs. Beginning as the producer of
animated shorts, he parlayed the success of his
first feature-length cartoon, *Snow White & The
Seven Dwarfs* (1938), into an animation empire
that soon included his own studio, the syndi-
cated *Mickey Mouse Club*, a weekly TV series
on NBC, and the Disneyland theme park. But
while he employed hundreds, Disney jealously
guarded his power, ruling his magic kingdom
with absolute authority. As a result, when he
died of cancer in 1966, his company suffered
serious disruptions. Although Disney World
in Florida was an initial success, its failing motion picture division nearly sent the company
into bankruptcy. Creatively rudderless, the
company spent nearly two decades in financial
limbo until the board hired Michael Eisner and
Jeffrey Katzenberg away from Paramount in
1984.

● When you think of innovative electronics, do
you ever think of Sony? Thirty years ago, the
manufacturing giant was the leader in consumer electronics. The Trinitron color television,
Walkman personal audio device, and PlaySta-
tion video game system made Sony synonymous with cutting-edge home and personal
entertainment. But when its visionary founder,
Akio Morita, stepped down as chairman in

1994, this company also went into a creative decline. With no comparable innovator to take the helm, Sony could only spin its wheels, producing variations on its past products, and losing market share as a result. Today, Sony is just another TV and digital camera manufacturer among dozens, its name more familiar to 21st century consumers as a motion picture studio than as a "must have" personal electronics brand.

● Howard Schultz didn't found Starbucks, but he was responsible for the coffee retailer's amazing growth when he served as chairman and CEO from 1986 to 2000. Shultz helped take the company public in 1992, and, when he left the chairmanship, Starbucks was already the world's largest coffee-house chain. Although an accomplished CFO, Schultz's successor, Orin Smith, lacked Schultz's passion and imagination. As a result, shares in Starbucks plummeted 50 percent under Smith's administration. Fortunately, Schultz returned to Starbucks in 2008 and for the next five years instituted aggressive expansions that once again cemented the company's market primacy, a position it holds today.

. . .

Of course, staging a successful succession is not just a challenge for major corporations. Smaller companies (like cannabusinesses) can be vulnerable if a founder/owner has not prepared for their sudden departure. In 2013, researchers at the University of Bergen in Norway released a study concerning the fortunes of 341 privately held companies that were at least 10 years old when their majority owner/founder died. (Norway happens to keep very good records on such things.) The researchers found that:

- On average, sales dropped by 60 percent in the four years after the owner's death.

- Two years after an owner's death, the survival rate for companies was 20 percent lower than for those where the owner was still living.

- The risk of bankruptcy was significantly higher for businesses whose original owners had recently passed.

So how can you ensure your company will endure should you no longer be at the helm, either by choice or happenstance? Steps to take right now include:

- If you don't have one already, create a company operations manual detailing every aspect of your company's activities. It should be a "How-To" manual for running your cannabusiness, no matter *who* is in charge.

- Buy "keyman insurance." This is a special life insurance policy ensuring your company remains solvent in the event of your sudden demise.

- Choose a strong second-in-command/successor who can take charge in your absence. Make sure this person is not only properly trained but also shares your vision and passion for the business you created.

- Make sure everyone in your organization recognizes your designated heir as your legitimate successor. To assist, put him/her in charge when you take time off to make others comfortable with their authority and management style.

- Pick two or three other top performers to serve as backups. They, too, should become intimately familiar with all aspects of your operations and share your vision for your company's future. Tell them, "I can only invest my time in so many people, but I want to invest it in you because I see something in you." These are magic words.

- Encourage your direct reports to do the same for members of the team.

* * *

Beyond this advice, we recommend *not* hiding your intentions. Inform candidates what you're doing—*and why*. Doing so will get/keep them invested in the process, benefitting you and your company. But please know, growing your people isn't something you can do in a few minutes. It takes time.

This was a lesson learned late by a cannabusiness founder we'll call Sam. Sam had always been a go-it-alone kind of guy. He spent his 20s growing his cannabusiness. It was his passion—okay, his obsession.

Yet Sam never took the time to think about growing *his people*. He just assumed he would always be in power. Tragically, soon after his 39th birthday, Sam was diagnosed with terminal cancer. Because his business sustained his family (wife and two kids), he knew he needed it to continue to provide for them.

For the next few months, he played catch-up, doing what he should have done years ago. Beyond spending time with his family, he concentrated on developing several people to take the reins once he passed away to not only ensure the business wouldn't go under, but that it would continue his legacy.

Certainly, you needn't be in such a desperate situation to come to this conclusion, but the lesson still holds: being powerful means also growing your people, empowering them to help *you* lead.

## POWER HOMEWORK

Use your journal to reflect on the following questions and act on suggestions.

1. Who are the people on your team you want to help develop their power? Be specific: Whom should you invest your time and money in? (Note: if you can't find people to invest with power, you've hired the wrong people.)

2. Talk with these people about power, informing them you want them to develop theirs. Ask how they feel about power and whether they want to hone this muscle.

3. What decisions will you allow these people to make? List them.

4. Better yet, ask these people to advocate for those decisions they would like to make.

5. Create a plan or an approach for what you will do if any of these people abuse or misuse their power.

# *Chapter*

# YOU BREAK IT, YOU OWN IT

An old saying tells us that some people are born to power, while others have power thrust upon them. (In the cannabusiness, most of us are the latter.) Another adage tells us true character is best revealed under pressure. Anyone can look like a hero when things are going well; it's when things are going wrong—sometimes, horribly wrong—that is the true test of one's mettle.

President Harry S. Truman, who assumed office following the death of Franklin Delano Roosevelt on April 12, 1945, faced some of the most harrowing decisions ever demanded of an American Commander-in-Chief. Not only did Truman have to shepherd American forces during the final months of World War II, he, and he alone, had to greenlight the dropping of atomic bombs on Japan. This was a decision he knew would result in the deaths of tens of thousands of civilians.

Despite all of this, Truman made no bones about the burdens of presidential authority. Knowing his position made him an easy target for critics, his folksy response was,

"If you can't stand the heat, get out of the kitchen." He also kept a wooden sign on his desk proclaiming: "The buck stops here."

"Passing the buck" is an expression meaning "shifting responsibility for something to somebody else." Scholars believe it has its roots in poker played by frontiersmen in the 19th century. In the Old West, poker players often used an object, like a buckhorn-handled knife, as a marker to indicate the dealer in a particular hand. If someone preferred not to assume this responsibility, he would—literally—"pass the buck" to another player.

But back to Truman. As an experienced politician, he knew responsibility is not something an effective leader can abdicate. As he stated in an address to the National War College in 1952, "You know, it's easy for the Monday morning quarterback to say what the coach should have done after the game is over. But when the decision is up before you—and on my desk I have a motto which says, 'The Buck Stops Here'—the decision has to be made."

In his farewell address in January 1953, Truman again raised this issue. "The President—whoever he is—has to decide. He can't pass the buck to anybody. No one else can do the deciding for him. That's his job."

As a cannabusiness owner or CEO, you—and you alone—are responsible for all that occurs in your organization. This includes both the good *and* the bad. Like they say at Pottery Barn, "You break it, you bought it."

But what does "taking responsibility" actually mean? Like so many buzzwords, "responsibility" is a term that gets bandied about so often, it loses its meaning. You are right to ask: What does a business owner need to do specifically to "take responsibility"?

Here are five markers of what "taking responsibility" actually means:

1. **STAYING AWARE** of activities at every level of your organization. Responsible leaders keep an eye on operations and interactions from the C-Suite all the way down to administrative support and maintenance. Just as "ignorance of the law is no excuse," when it comes to criminal defense, claiming to be unaware of events outside your purview because "It's not my department" shows a lack of accountability.

2. **TAKING ACTIONS** to fix problems before they become crises. Finding and applying solutions can be hard. Which is why many people's instinct is to ignore issues, hoping they "go away on their own." In fact, like a paper cut, some problems do "heal" without outside intervention. But sometimes the paper cut can get infected. And that infection can spread into the bloodstream, leading to sepsis—and death. A responsible leader understands the threat even seemingly minor problems pose and takes action to stem them before they become catastrophes.

Along these lines, let's consider a cautionary tale. At a cannabis organization there was once a CEO we will call

Dennis. Dennis allowed a toxic culture to fester until it became a systemic infection. One of his employees, Mark, was an out gay man with a husband. His direct manager, Kenneth, not only made snarky comments to Mark's face, but instigated hurtful gossip. Taking cues from Kenneth, other managers and employees would openly talk disparagingly about Mark.

Over time, other staff learned how Mark was being treated and revolted. They questioned Dennis's ability to lead. After all, Kenneth's actions did not happen in a vacuum. If Dennis knew about this, he was complicit (even in his silence.) If he did *not know* about it, it demonstrated cluelessness.

3. **SEEKING SOLUTIONS** instead of blaming others. When things go south, one's instinct is to accuse someone else. In a business environment, finger-pointing, especially the kind driven by self-preservation, leads to breakdowns in personal relationships, diminished morale, organizational paranoia, and yet even more failures. A responsible leader first acknowledges a problem exists, then says, "How can we ensure something like this never happens again?" (The truth is most big failures are the result of myriad smaller failures combining to create a cascade effect. Rarely is it because Person X took Action Z.)

4. **MAKING PERSONAL** sacrifices. Being "the Boss" entails doing what it takes to make sure

a job gets done. This can mean working longer hours, sometimes missing important family events, and even cutting your own pay to make payroll.

Here's another cautionary tale on this topic. On January 13, 2012, the Italian cruise ship *Concordia* struck rocks off the coast of Giglio Island in the Tyrrhenian Sea and capsized. The captain, Francesco Schettino, not only violated protocols by taking his vessel too close to shore, but he also committed the ultimate sin of abandoning his post and hopping into one of the first lifeboats.

By ignoring the cardinal rule of command—a captain should be the last person off a sinking ship—Schettino proved himself to be not only incompetent but a coward. Thirty-two people died due to his incompetence, and the jury in his manslaughter trial had little sympathy for the man. He was found guilty on all counts and sentenced to 16 years in prison. Had Schettino attended to the safety of his passengers and taken responsibility for his actions, his punishment likely would have been far less severe.

5. **BEING ABLE** to take criticism. If you're expecting everyone to applaud you, it's time for some cold water. As a leader, you can expect the exact opposite of what you would get in a personal relationship: less positive feedback and more criticism. More bad news than good news. To be a responsible leader requires thick skin. It also means taking the hits as they come, then learning from experiences to prevent

similar failures from ever occurring. It's key not to pat yourself on the back for the good things, but rather, to own the bad. Above all else, in the face of so much negativity, stay strong.

But there's one more application to responsibility. And it's a key one. As we have said, responsible leaders understand they can't do it all alone. Work needs to be *delegated*. Responsibility must be *shared* for a business to thrive. Only, here's the catch: it needs to be shared with the *right* people.

Anyone who has studied business theory has likely heard the phrase "You need to put the right people on the bus and make sure they're sitting in the right seats." This is an easy metaphor to visualize, but it's a misleading one.

On a bus, there are no "right" seats and "wrong" seats. That's because bus passengers are passive. They have no input into the vehicle's operations. Passengers can sit where they damned well please, and, as long as the driver does their job, the bus will get where it's supposed to go.

Instead of a bus, we prefer the analogy of an old-fashioned cargo ship. On it, everyone has a job. The helmsman steers the vessel. The chief engineer maintains the engines. The radarman scans for approaching ships. The chief cook runs the galley and makes sure everyone is fed on time. And it's all overseen by a captain.

Now, a good captain would never dream of placing an engineer in charge of the galley or asking the cook to manage the engine room. Everyone has their area of responsibility. It's the captain's role to ensure everyone does theirs.

Likewise, a good CEO finds talented people and assigns

them to the tasks for which they are best qualified. Even though employees may have certain freedoms, responsibility *always* comes back to the person at the top.

Like the sign on Truman's desk once said, "The buck stops here."

## POWER HOMEWORK

Using your journal, address the following:

1. Do you feel you're responsible for the work produced in your business, or do you feel it's someone else's problem? Why?

2. Do you take credit for good outcomes and place blame on others when things go badly?

3. What do you do to encourage a sense of responsibility within individuals on your team?

4. What steps have you taken to inadvertently or deliberately undercut a sense of responsibility?

5. Ask people on your team whether they feel responsible for the organizational outcomes your business is facing. If not, ask them why and specifically what, if anything, you've done to encourage this feeling.

# PART 3

# POWER

*and*

# COMMUNICATION

# Chapter

# DON'T JUST MAKE DECISIONS, SPREAD DECISION-MAKING

To increase your power, it's key to utilize other decision-makers in your organization to spread your message. Let's go to the movies to see this idea in action. In the 1978 classic *Superman: The Movie*, Lex Luthor (Gene Hackman) launches two stolen nuclear-tipped ICBMs, one heading east, one west. Superman (Christopher Reeve), just released from kryptonite bondage by Luthor's assistant Eve Teschmacher (Valerie Perrine), must pick which missile to pursue. He intercepts the eastbound rocket, hurling it harmlessly into space. But the westbound rocket hits its target, the blast rupturing California's San Andreas Fault, causing catastrophic damage up and down the West Coast.

Because he and he *alone* had the power to stop the missiles, Superman was left with an impossible choice. No matter which missile he stopped, the other would get through and millions would die. Sadly, even the vaunted Man of Steel cannot be in two places at once.

Many an entrepreneur and CEO sees himself or herself as a superhero. They believe they reached the pinnacle of success by having "powers and abilities far beyond those of mortal men—and women." Cast in the role of supreme leader, they resist sharing power with others they view as inferiors. There's a flip side to the disdain some leaders show for those who don't "get it" and therefore can't be entrusted with power. These same leaders are often afraid if they do entrust someone with power this person will somehow screw things up, making it even more difficult for the leader and the company to succeed.

In fact, most leaders *do* possess an enhanced degree of intelligence, skill, experience, and/or charisma that allowed them to reach their lofty positions in the first place. But, like Superman, no one—no matter how capable—can be in two places at once. No one can also control *everything* that happens in a company. And the larger the organization, the harder it becomes to function. At some point, a leader wishing to grow must cede some authority. They must learn to *delegate* and, if they're really brave, enable people to *advocate* for decisions they'd like to make. (Though we covered this topic in previous chapters, there is more to say about it in terms of how delegating to others and encouraging self-advocacy can actually grow your people and your power.)

Now, if you find delegation and promoting self-advocacy difficult, you're not alone. Most entrepreneurs live by the adage, "If you want something done right, do it yourself." But as discussed, keeping all authority to oneself can be self-defeating. Something critical *will* get overlooked.

Something important will go unattended. One errant missile will get through and shatter the San Andreas Fault.

Trying to control every aspect of a growing company can also be exhausting, both physically and mentally. Over time, the stress of command will wear at one's psyche. Without relief, even the toughest among us will crack. And when that happens, the entire company can go down as well.

In addition to the fact that limits exist to what any one human can accomplish in any given day, there are two other, equally compelling reasons to practice delegation and foster self-advocacy for your team. The first is, people given power by an authority necessarily recognize the *source* of that authority, increasing the leader's power.

Here's an example. In the medieval feudal system, kings granted degrees of autonomy to their vassals who, in turn, granted smaller degrees of autonomy to *their* vassals. This system survived for 1,000 years because everybody recognized that while power flowed downward, authority flowed *upward*. The king was still the kingdom's Big Cheese. He literally held the power of life or death over everyone below him.

The second reason delegation and self-advocacy grows your power is, when people are given decision-making authority, or advocate for it, they acquire a vested interest in the operation's success. They become more proactive, more engaged, more creative, and more productive. They even begin to see the business as not just a place to work, but as an extension of themselves.

Organizations seeking greatness must transition from an order-taker mentality to an *intrapreneurial* mentality. After all, granting your employees more say in decisions doesn't limit one's power, it *increases* it by making others feel like they have a stake in your success.

Just to be clear, there is a world of difference between delegation and self-advocacy. The former is when someone with power gives someone else with less power something to do (signifying presumed authority). The latter concerns allowing the space/structure whereby power is known and clear so members of your team can advocate for their own desires to make decisions (while serving the organization's greater good). Self-advocacy is a higher form of empowerment than delegation, but both have their value.

Knowing the difference between these two tactics is essential. Once you determine those from your team who want to make decisions, empower them to do so. Shift decision-making to these individuals to benefit your organization, expanding your power. Also, delegating and promoting self-advocacy aren't things you just *do*. Like all aspects of company operations, they require careful planning, execution, and oversight. Basic tips include:

### 1. KNOW WHAT TASKS CAN *AND* CAN'T BE DELEGATED OR ADVOCATED FOR.

Generally, effective leaders reserve strategic decisions for themselves, while delegating tactical decisions and implementation to subordinates. What's the difference between strategy and tactics? Simply put, strategy is *what* you choose to do. Tactics are *how* you choose to do it. Another way to look at it: as leader, you should be the "Big Picture" person. You choose the objectives. You set the rules. You establish a timetable and benchmarks for success. You then leave the pesky "details" to your staff.

## 2. UNDERSTAND YOUR EMPLOYEE'S STRENGTHS AND WEAKNESSES.

*Who* you choose to delegate *to* is just as important as the tasks you choose to delegate. You must make sure the people you entrust with assignments have the skills, training, experience, and temperaments to see them through. Some people have natural leadership abilities while, sadly, others do not. Likewise, some people are self-starters while others need direction. As company leader, you know—or *should* know—your people better than anyone and thus fit each job with the most qualified individual.

## 3. ARTICULATE THE OUTCOMES YOU EXPECT TO ACHIEVE.

When delegating, it's crucial to let your subordinates know exactly what you expect from them. Tell them the results you want to see and when you want to see them. And then . . . let them do their thing. The whole point of delegating is to *let go*.

## 4. PROVIDE THE NECESSARY TOOLS.

Just as carpenters can't do their jobs without their hammers, saws, rulers, and screwdrivers, managers and employees at every level need the proper implements to deliver the results you demand. It's your job to make sure they have them. Depending on the nature of your business, this can include physical space, technology, software, training, support, and personnel.

## 5. SET UP PROPER COMMUNICATIONS CHANNELS.

Communication is always a two-way street. You must establish protocols for communicating with your subordinates, and for them to converse with you. Make it easy for them to ask questions, request clarification, or get further directions. Also, meet regularly so you can get progress updates and make operational adjustments as needed.

## 6. ALLOW FOR A LEARNING CURVE.

The people to whom you delegate are unlikely to hit the ground running. Most will need time to adjust to their new responsibilities, and they will make mistakes. Subordinates must feel free to fail (on occasion) without risking your wrath. In fact, failure is often the best teacher.

## 7. DON'T UNDERCUT THE AUTHORITY OF OTHERS.

Nothing's worse than a leader who delegates jobs but then proceeds to micromanage subordinates every step along the way. Hovering over direct reports like a helicopter parent undermines the reason for delegating in the first place. Worse, it demoralizes the people you have delegated *to*. Trust the people you have hired. And if you don't trust them, you shouldn't have selected them in the first place.

• • •

The following stories illustrate the value of delegation, self-advocacy, and the price you pay for avoiding these empowering practices. In the first case, there once was a small cannabis retail business founded by a bright entrepreneur. Although Tom was great at his job, he was a perfectionist and demanded things always be done "his way."

Interested in expanding his business, he called in a well-known consultant who suggested Tom hire a manager to run the store while he focused on expansion. After interviewing candidates, Tom chose a "Number One" with the experience and temperament he sought.

But after a few days, Tom got antsy and returned to his old ways, micromanaging every aspect of his company's operations. Feeling impotent, the manager quit, and Tom resumed his place as both CEO and COO. The store continued to make money, but it never grew in either volume or profitability.

In a nearby city, a similar narrative was unfolding. This company, too, was headed a compulsive micromanager, Sharon, who hired a manager based on the advice of a consultant. In this case, it was to handle distribution.

Evan, the new manager, came with a whole list of suggestions and ideas to grow the business and make it more profitable. But Sharon was different than her counterpart.

She saw *value* in what Evan offered and gave him the autonomy to implement his concepts. In just a few months, Evan completely transformed Sharon's business.

Due to Evan's contributions, Sharon's company took on far more volume. They were able to expand their white label business and bring in more product from growers, all because they established a structure of internal empowerment. And because Sharon stopped micromanaging.

Of course, Sharon was concerned at first about giving her new hire so much power. But she couldn't argue with the measurable benefits. In time, and due to her forward thinking, her business became the largest in its market.

All too often, people don't invest in others, thinking it will strip their power. Senior people are often comfortable continuing to make middle-level decisions when they should be letting their employees do it. Just as you are growing cannabis, you need to grow your *people*. It's the only true way to powerfully scale.

## POWER HOMEWORK

Get that journal out again and reflect on these questions:

1. Are you willing to give up power and decision-making to grow your company?

2. Drill down. What important decisions do you want to make? What important decisions would you be comfortable with *others* making?

3. Do you find it hard to let go of power and decision-making? If so, why is that the case?

4. Do you have people on your team you trust to make decisions? Who are they? Write their names down.

5. What steps are you taking to give these people more responsibiliy and to make them better decision-makers? What opportunities are you providing them to make real and substantive decisions?

*Chapter*

# DON'T JUST GIVE FEEDBACK, TAKE IT

You can't manage an organization without reliable data. Yet, when you're at the top of a hierarchical pyramid, reliable information can be hard to come by, especially when it's intelligence about *your own performance*.

One of the paradoxes of power is the more you have, the less you can trust others to tell you the truth. Example: most subordinates are reluctant to tell their boss they're making poor decisions, that they're mismanaging the organization, or behaving in inappropriate or counterproductive ways.

Having done the calculus, most subordinates realize there's far more to gain by currying favor with the boss, by stroking their ego with flattery and praise, than by "speaking truth to power." (The cliché of the incompetent "Big Boss" surrounded by fawning "Yes Men" is based on this unfortunate reality.)

Wise leaders recognize this problem and take steps to address it. Kings and emperors would sometimes leave their protected confines dressed as "common folk" to circulate among the locals and learn what people were really saying about their rule.

Sweden's King Charles XI (1672–1697) gained significant notoriety for doing just that. Abandoning courtiers and sycophants at his palace, he lived among his subjects for weeks at a time so he could better gauge his performance and that of his government. (His nickname, "Grey Coat," was derived from the simple, unassuming attire he would wear during his forays among the country's hoi polloi.)

So how can *you* gauge your own performance? Aside from donning a wig, gluing on a fake nose, and joining your workforce *Undercover Boss*–style, there are a few simple—but essential—steps you can take to get an honest, 360-degree view of your own effectiveness.

First among these is to set up a formal two-way feedback system. As noted, most companies are structured as a traditional pyramid, with the leader at the top and various ranks arranged below in an expanding fashion. Like water running down a hill, information tends to flow from the top down. Managers *give* orders, they *give* direction, and they *give* criticism, but they rarely, if ever *take* any of these— except from the people above them.

Of course, if you're at the top of the heap, well, then you have no one giving you orders or direction—and especially criticism. This arrangement can be pleasant, but it's likely to also give you a false sense of security. Too often, rulers are often blithely unaware of grumbling in the ranks until one day a mob shows up armed with torches and pitchforks.

In other words, soliciting feedback from subordinates is

a necessary and important mechanism. To this end, studies show effective two-way communication can deliver four principal benefits to any business:

### 1. GREATER EMPLOYEE JOB SATISFACTION.

Workers feel better about their jobs and themselves when you offer them a way to express their concerns, ideas, opinions, and suggestions.

### 2. ENHANCED PRODUCTIVITY.

Two-way feedback helps reduce ambiguity about people's roles and responsibilities.

### 3. GREATER INNOVATION.

Collaboration between team members at all levels supports creativity and the sharing of ideas.

### 4. GREATER TRUST.

When workers see leadership values them, it creates greater loyalty, job retention, and opportunities for growth.

At this point, you may be bristling at the notion of regularly soliciting feedback from subordinates. You might be thinking, "This is my company, and I will run it the way *I* see fit. A business isn't a democracy. If some people don't like the way I do things, they're free to look for jobs elsewhere."

Examples abound of business owners and CEOs who rule their capitalist kingdoms like this, with iron fists reminiscent of Third World dictators. Some even prosper using this "My Way or the Highway" approach.

But if you're truly interested in maximizing your power—and that *is* what this book is about—then demanding unquestioned fealty like some modern-day Chairman Mao is like flying a 747 jumbo jet on just one engine. You may eventually get to your destination, but the journey is going to be sluggish, your controls not fully responsive.

The truth is your staff members aren't mere tools for you to manipulate at will; they are *assets* who know things and see things you cannot—and never will. Combine their perspectives with yours and you will know more and be able to do more than you ever could alone. (No matter how smart you are, you will never have the IQ of your aggregate team!)

Seeking honest feedback? You must allow your people to be critical of you without fear of retribution. To use a modern buzzword, you must create a "safe space" where they are free to express the truth as they see it without risking their jobs or chances for advancement. You might even *incentivize* criticism if it's constructive with cash bonuses, time off, or other perks to pry such critiques from otherwise reluctant mouths. Make it a safe game to tell the boss the truth.

You must also understand your workers are your allies, not your adversaries. (And if they're not your allies, why are they there?) This is particularly true of people working in the cannabis industry. Few people go into this business just because they need a *job*. They do it because they are passionate about the product and the lifestyle it represents. They want to be involved in something they believe in and are willing to sacrifice much to see it succeed.

It's also key to understand this: when workers offer criticism, it's rarely out of pure self-interest, but out of a great love for the calling to which they have devoted their lives. You want to encourage this kind of engagement.

So, if two-way feedback *is* useful, why do so many powerful people avoid soliciting it? One big reason is fear of appearing vulnerable. Many leaders view a willingness to accept criticism as a sign of weakness and inviting negative feedback as an invitation to insurrection.

This is a mistake. In truth, the most powerful stand to benefit from being vulnerable. In fact, vulnerability can actually be an *asset* when it comes to accumulating and maintaining power.

Dr. Brené Brown is an American researcher and educator who has spent years studying this subject. A visiting professor in management at the McCombs School of Business at the University of Texas at Austin, she's the author of five *New York Times* number-one best-sellers, including *The Gifts of Imperfection*, *Daring Greatly*, *Rising Strong*, *Braving the Wilderness*, and *Dare to Lead*. Her 2011 TED Talk, "The Power of Vulnerability," has been viewed more than 15 million times.

In her work, Brown offers observations on the power of vulnerability. Some of her major quotes include: "Vulnerability is not about winning or losing; it's having the courage to show up and be seen when we have no control over the outcome," "In our culture, we associate vulnerability with emotions we want to avoid such as fear, shame, and uncertainty. Yet we too often lose sight of the fact that vulnerability is also the birthplace of joy, belonging, creativity, authenticity, and love," and "When you shut down vulnerability, you shut down opportunity."

Like everything in business, an effective two-way feedback system doesn't just *happen*. It needs to be carefully designed, implemented, and maintained. Crucial components of such a program include these prescriptives:

◈ **MAKE IT PART OF YOUR HIRING PROCESS.**
Don't just seek "order-takers." You want people who are motivated, who are always on the lookout for new solutions, who are life-long learners, and who aren't afraid to speak their minds.

◈ **PROVIDE FEEDBACK TRAINING.**
Most employees and leaders have little or no experience with two-way feedback and may need practice making it work. There's a right and a wrong way to do it. Working with a business communications consultant experienced in such matters may prove useful, especially at the beginning.

◈ **WHEN FEEDBACK IS OFFERED, DON'T BE DEFENSIVE.**
When Steve was at Apple, feedback was often "offered," and people were encouraged to take it. A favorite expression bandied about hallways was, "Shut up and take the feedback." The culture had no patience for those unwilling to take criticism or instruction. You also had to take it in without defensiveness. People had

to see you "got it" even if you didn't embrace their perspective.

● **ESTABLISH CLEAR EXPECTATIONS AND BOUNDARIES.**
Two-way feedback shouldn't be a free-for-all. You need to establish rules and enforce them.

● **MAKE IT ROUTINE.**
The idea of the "yearly progress report" went out the window years ago. Feedback needs to be ongoing and regular. Make it part of your company culture.

● **SHOW OFF YOUR RESULTS.**
Making two-way feedback work requires, well, *feedback*. When workers see their input is leading to concrete results, they're more apt to stay invested in the process.

So come out from behind your lead shield. It won't protect you so much as isolate you. Instead, get ahead of what others think by soliciting candid feedback. Receiving this information won't hurt you. It will help you grow, improving your organization and growing your power.

## POWER HOMEWORK

Get that journal out again to consider these questions:

1. Are you willing to give *and* receive feedback to grow your company?

2. What makes you uncomfortable about receiving feedback from subordinates?

3. Do you have people on your team you trust to provide you feedback? Who are they? Write their names down.

4. What steps can you take to get feedback from these people? How can you encourage them to offer it?

5. How can you lower your defensiveness when receiving feedback—especially feedback you don't like?

# Chapter

# USE YOUR WORDS CAREFULLY AND OFTEN

We've been taught actions speak louder than words. But when it comes to exercising power, words are some of the most powerful tools you wield.

William Shakespeare's 18th play, *Henry V*, was first performed at London's Globe Theatre around 1599. Based on the exploits of the real 15th century monarch, Henry takes a small army across the English Channel to fight the French and seize the disputed crown. On the fields near the French town of Agincourt, Henry realizes his forces are badly outnumbered, his chances of victory slim.

But Henry is not one to give up. As Shakespeare tells the story, Henry gathered his troops and, flush with inspiration, gives the following speech:

> "From this day to the ending of the world,
> But we in it shall be remembered—
> We few, we happy few, we band of brothers;

For he to-day that sheds his blood with me
Shall be my brother; be he ne'er so vile,
This day shall gentle his condition;
And gentlemen in England now a-bed
Shall think themselves accurs'd they were not
    here,
And hold their manhoods cheap whiles any
    speaks
That fought with us upon Saint Crispin's day."

Read the above passage carefully. The prose is 400+ years old yet still resonates and inspires. What Henry is telling his beleaguered army is that "If you fight with me today, you will be exalted above all others—and if you win, you will have truly done something incredible."

Those in England who are not with us, says Henry in Shakespeare's telling, "Will hold their manhoods cheap." Those who fight with me, says Henry, "We few, we happy few, we band of brothers; For he to-day that sheds his blood with me shall be my brother" and always be remembered.

Inspired by Henry's words, dismal French military tactics, and the superiority of English longbows, Henry's troops, though outnumbered, conquer the more numerous French forces, allowing Henry to take the crown.

Now, it's certainly possible to look at Henry's speech as another example of someone who has power exhorting those who don't, to support his efforts. This might very well be true, but in the end, Henry's army wanted to prevail because failure meant death and humiliation. It might have meant the end of England. They wanted to win, and this statement by Henry played a big part in driving them to victory.

In modern fiction, we find more scenes of leaders, under intense pressure, rallying their troops through inspirational rhetoric. From John "Bluto" Blutarsky's absurd "Was it over when the Germans bombed Pearl Harbor?" harangue in *Animal House*, to President Thomas Whitmore's stirring "Today we celebrate our Independence Day!" oration in *Independence Day*, great leaders find they can overcome even the longest odds through inspirational words and passionate delivery to create a vision of success.

Fortunately, the real world has plenty of great orators too. In Steve's lifetime, he has had the pleasure of watching some of the greatest speakers of the 20th and 21st centuries capturing and inspiring audiences with stirring language and electrifying declamation.

But great rhetoric is not the sole province of politicians, motivational speakers, and world-renowned captains of industry or the military. Even leaders of small businesses can—and should—use the power of their words to build, strengthen, and inspire their teams. (It's never enough to just give orders and issue directives. You must light a fire in the hearts of your people, stirring them to action!)

That's why it's troubling how so many leaders fail to see the benefit of using their voices. They don't see the value of regular, inspirational communication. Their perspective is "I'm busy. Why bother? My people will do what I ask them to do when I ask them to do it."

But *will they?* Not if you haven't committed to the exercise of regular and powerful communication.

What's more, good communication *enhances* power. That's why every head of state employs communications directors and professional speechwriters. Authoritarian regimes often establish *entire departments* dedicated to what became known in the early 20th century as "propaganda," which, despite its modern negative connotation, is derived from the word *propagate*, or "to spread." (In this case, tailored information.)

Today, in a professional setting, communication is more than just making an occasional announcement about a new hire, an updated company policy, or reminding people about casual Fridays. Communication should be used to repeatedly paint a vision of where the company is going and how you plan to get there.

Accordingly, you need to tell a story people can latch on to and be inspired by. It must focus on your company's purpose, the benefits you are all working to deliver, and, from the employee standpoint, what's in it for *them*. (While rewards can include money, they should also include intangibles, such as pride, happiness, and satisfaction.) If you can do all of this, you will enhance their belief in you and, as a result, increase your power.

And if enhancing your power isn't a good enough reason to communicate, studies have shown the most productive employees are those who are most engaged. They feel this way by understanding where you're leading them. And they glean where you're leading them by being exposed to a systematic campaign of communication.

The key to a successful communications campaign is *consistency*. It's through frequent exposure to concepts and plans that we develop familiarity. Plan to speak directly to your team at least once a week, either in person or, if that's not possible, virtually. You don't want to be viewed as a distant, mysterious figure tucking away in an ivory tower, but as a "fighting general" who is in the "trenches" with your troops.

Another key element of successful communication is honesty. You need to share the bad news as well as the good. Being upfront about negative events makes you look credible and worthy of the power with which you have been entrusted. Speaking from a vulnerable position can also actually work to your benefit, as people like King Henry V, Notre Dame head coach Knute Rockne, and even "Bluto" Blutarsky can attest; the best inspirational speeches are always delivered when things seem their bleakest.

Steve's old boss, Apple co-founder and CEO Steve Jobs, was a master orator. Steve was lucky enough to see Jobs's speaking abilities up close on several occasions. His introduction of the Macintosh computer on January 24, 1984, is the stuff of legend. The video of this event has, as of this writing, had more than 9.5 million views on YouTube.

Jobs always made public speaking look easy, but he worked hard on his major presentations. Knowing he had just this one chance to share his awesome vision with the world and rouse his workers into action, he spent weeks preparing his speech, rewriting until the last possible minute to ensure every word was just right.

"Watching Jobs present that day gave me goosebumps. He was so sure of his vision, so committed to its execution that we, his team, thought, despite all that was in our way, we would prevail," says Steve. "His presentation style filled me with awe. He connected with people. You were *proud* to be with him. You had no doubt you were changing the world!"

In this way, Jobs was like Shakespeare's Henry V. Through words and presentation, he created a grand, shared vision. He bonded his people together as one and made them feel invincible. And because he made them feel that way, they were.

Listen to Malala Yousafzai's Nobel Peace Prize acceptance speech for another example of stirring rhetoric. She's clear. She's passionate. She's fearless. She advocates for the universal education of children and equal rights for women.

Possessing a clear message, she invites her audience to participate in her quest. It's memorable. It's passionate. It's direct. She decided to speak up and not accept the injustices of the Taliban. She identified herself with the 66 million girls around the world who are not allowed to be educated and are abused. Without hesitation, Yousafzai said, "This shall not stand."

Of course, effective communication doesn't just "happen." Communication must be planned and executed with a strategy in mind. It must have a specific purpose, and every communication you create must serve that purpose.

This means there are no "throwaway" messages. No "just spinning our wheels" missives. Every time you get up in front of your employees you are either adding or subtracting from your credibility. You're either enhancing or diminishing your power. If you seem disinterested or halfhearted in your messaging, your receivers will respond in kind. If you seem fearful, you will also engender fear in your listeners. And if you callously embarrass or scold people, they will remember that and little else.

Bear in mind communication takes place on multiple levels. A popular expression today is "content is king," but substance alone—no matter how well-crafted—may not produce the kind of reaction you seek. This is because communication is about more than information. It's about more than even ideas. Effective communication is about *emotion*. As the late poet Maya Angelou put it, "People will forget what you said, people will forget what you did, but people will never forget how you made them *feel*."

To this point, have you ever attended a concert and felt like you were on a higher plane? You may not remember half the songs you heard, but you know the experience made you feel great. Or did you ever see a great comedian perform and laugh so hard your face literally hurt? You probably don't remember most of the jokes, but you sure as hell know you had a great time.

That's the effect you want to go for. When you speak, you must speak with passion. You must orate with conviction. You must talk with drama. You want to transfer your excitement, your optimism, and your enthusiasm to your listeners. You want to make them *believe* in your vision as strongly as you do, to feel the same giddy enthusiasm that makes you want to get out of bed every morning.

No one wants to work for a boring company. So, find a way to tap your people's passions by stating audacious yet achievable goals. Also, use your communication efforts to laud people who achieve their aims.

To summarize, here are tips for communicating to motivate others:

1. Be clear on what you want to accomplish. No one will follow a person whose goals constantly shift.

2. Tell a larger story. Infuse pride into your communication. Make people feel special for joining your cause.

3. Make your team feel proud to be with you.

4. Tell the bad news as well as the good news.

5. Be honest, every time.

6. Communicate regularly—not just when something big happens.

7. Be prepared when you speak. Have a message and a call to action. Every time.

Ultimately, your communication prowess will either enhance your power or destroy it. Which will it be for you?

## POWER HOMEWORK

Get your journal out to address these questions:

1. What hesitations do you have about communicating with your team?

2. What do you experience when you talk to your

people? Are they listening closely or are they distracted? Are they inspired or bored?

**3.** Do you have set of topics you want to cover when you speak, or do you just wing it?

**4.** Moving forward, think about the messages you want to communicate and how they support your vision. Don't waste the time of your people by getting up and droning on about trivialities. Each communication effort should be treated as a golden opportunity to move people to action, not bore them. They're golden opportunities to reinforce your vision.

PART 4

# POWER

*and*

# VISION

*Chapter*

# IF YOU FAIL
# TO PLAN, YOU PLAN
# TO FAIL

So, you've followed along with our advice in the last three sections because you dream of creating a famous brand and riding it to market dominance. *Great!* But becoming the next cannabusiness millionaire is going to take more than just aspirations, regardless of how attractive they may be.

It's even going to take more than those old work ethic standbys: dedication, hard work, and perseverance. No, to become powerful building a thriving company, you need a *vision* of what your company will be two, three, even five years from now. You must also create a specific *plan* to ensure you stay on track, a roadmap and timetable against which you can hold your team and yourself accountable.

Let your plans reflect and expand on your vision. (Plans that are unmoored from vision are not believable and will not inspire your team.) Instead, your vision should be laid down in a "vision statement."

Simply put, a vision statement is a short description,

usually a paragraph in length, painting a picture of what you expect your company to achieve long-term. If you are in cannabis production, how much volume do you hope to produce? If you're in cannabis retailing, how many locations do you envision operating? In what cities? States? What kind of dollar volume do you think you can ultimately achieve?

Unfortunately, some folks are reticent to commit their vision to paper. They think openly articulating their hopes and dreams will somehow "jinx" them, just as kids who blow out birthday cake candles are warned, "Don't tell anyone your wish, or it won't come true." Like the ancient Greeks who were punished for their hubris, they fear tempting the Fates.

Others believe our destinies are unknowable and unchangeable and we must be willing to simply "go with the flow." (As Doris Day once sang, "Que séra, séra—Whatever will be, will be.") Or they prefer to speak in only the most general of terms: "I want to create a successful cannabis business," or "I want to be a leader in the cannabis field," believing themselves to be "Big Picture" people who leave the details to others. Others are simply afraid to create a vision because they fear that the vision they articulate might be wrong and they'll be ridiculed. It's better for these people to just pretend it's not important.

The problem with this approach is, if you don't know where you're going, how will you know when you've arrived? Therefore, a vision statement must be as specific as possible, especially so you have something to measure your progress against. (As business managers like to say, "If you can't measure it, you can't manage it.")

To this end, it makes sense to speak in terms of *dollar volume*. *Staff size*. *Customer base*. Don't worry about being "wrong." You're painting a vision, not making a prediction. Even if you fail to meet, or better yet, exceed, your numbers, at least you'll know if you're moving in the right direction.

At this point, you may be wondering what differentiates a vision statement from a mission statement. The difference is, a mission statement lays out your company's purpose, *its reason for being*. A vision statement takes the mission and projects its intended results into the future. Ideally, a company's mission should not deviate over time. But what your company looks like today and what you hope it will look like a decade from now may—and probably *should*—be quite different.

So, the question is, how do you make your vision a reality? Simple: *Planning.*

Admittedly, many contradictory opinions exist on the value of long-term planning. Benjamin Franklin once said, "By failing to prepare, you prepare to fail." French author Antoine de Saint-Exupéry, best known for *The Little Prince*, noted, "A goal without a plan is just a wish." And President Dwight D. Eisenhower (then a general) stated, "In preparing for battle I have always found plans are useless, but planning is indispensable."

Unsurprisingly, life's complex and unpredictable nature has made others skeptical, even cynical, about the value of planning. Chaos theory, the 20th century mathematical model that became a pop culture meme thanks to the Michael Crichton 1990 novel *Jurassic Park*, posits, "Any sufficiently complex system is inherently unpredictable."

Former Beatle and songwriter John Lennon put it another way: "Life is what happens to you while you're busy making other plans." A century earlier, 19th Prussian general Helmuth von Moltke famously quipped, "No plan survives first contact with the enemy." There's even a Yiddish proverb that states simply: "Man plans. God laughs."

So much for fancy quotes. Think what you will about planning's value, but most companies fail quickly without one. Go into any bank for a loan and one of the first things they'll ask for is your business plan. (Yes, we only wish you could go to a bank for financing cannabis production and retailing, but even "friends and family" investors will also want to see a plan.)

To run a business without one is like hitting the road in an RV without a destination, map, or campsite reservation. True, you may stumble across some amazing sites and meet some extraordinary people, but you're just as likely to find yourself stuck in the middle of endless desert with no fuel, no water, and no place to dump your toilet waste.

Remember, a key part of business planning is anticipating where the market will be in a year, in three years, and in five, then adjusting your operations accordingly. Think about it like this: in basketball, you never throw the ball to where a teammate *is*. Instead, you throw it to where she's *going* to be in the next one or two seconds.

Likewise, when NASA sends a probe to Mars, they don't shoot the rocket to where Mars is *today*, but where they know Mars will be in the 18 or so months it will take the spacecraft to make the 194-million-mile journey. In a similar manner, you must *anticipate* market conditions months and even years out. Of course, unlike in astrophysics, you don't have proven mathematical formulas to follow. Instead, you must rely on research, expert opinions, historical trends, your own experience, as well as the expertise of your team.

What this means is, you need both a vision and a plan as guiding lights on your journey to business success. Without them, you are fumbling in the dark, hoping things will magically work out. (And as we're often admonished, "Hope is not a strategy.") Also, unless there is compelling evidence to the contrary, you need to stick to whatever plan you devise.

Sadly, many "leaders" in this business end up chasing "shiny objects." These are new ideas, sudden inspirations, and other fads that, like meteors, burn brightly for a few moments, then disappear in a puff of smoke.

Few of us have the fortitude to resist the siren's call of "the next big thing" to turn our original visions and plans into a reality. The problem is, if your company is constantly changing direction, reversing marketing strategies, trying to appeal to different customers with ever-changing product lines, it's a sure thing you and your team will suffer organizational and market whiplash.

Of course, sitting down to write a vision statement and business plan takes time. You may be saying to yourself, "I'm a busy person. I don't have time to write a business plan. We need to be taking action. Like *now*!" (This is akin to saying, "I don't have time to stop for gas. I have a critical business meeting to get to!") But unless you take time to prepare to get to where you wish to go, you may never get there at all.

So how do you stay the course? In the immortal words

of former First Lady Nancy Reagan: "Just say no." (Certainly, these words are not an expression of a coherent or beneficial drug policy, but it does have value for our discussion.)

But saying no is anathema to many entrepreneurs. They subscribe to the notion success is achieved by being as open-minded as possible, by always looking for new and exciting innovations, and having a positive, "Yes, I Can!" attitude toward all things.

This makes sense. As humans, we are constantly thrown alternatives that *appear* better than what we're doing. ("The grass is always greener on the other side of the hill.") But appearances can be deceiving. Rather than jump on every bandwagon that comes your way, hoping it will deliver huge dividends, it's better to be Aesop's Tortoise, moving slow and steady to win the race.

Don't get us wrong. Positivity is essential to success. If you didn't believe your business could succeed, you wouldn't bother founding it. And occasionally a new insight or discovery can have a hugely positive impact.

But compulsively saying yes to every new thing that comes along will inevitably lead you down blind alleys, draining you and your business of limited resources. As much as a positive attitude is imperative for success, so is discipline and stick-to-it-iveness. The death of many a fine company can be attributed to foolish leaders who chased the next bright, shiny object.

Don't make their mistake. Saying no makes you powerful. It's a discipline demonstrating you will not be distracted. You will focus on what matters.

As a leader, you have the ultimate power to show the

way forward with a compelling, defensible—even game-changing—vision/plan impacting hearts and minds. No one else can do this. Only you.

. . .

We're going to close this chapter by telling you another fairy tale. It's kind of like "The Three Little Pigs"—only it's "The Three Cannabis Guys." They came together to build a cannabis business. But one partner thought only about cultivation. He wanted to create the best possible product. The second was obsessed with creating an efficient manufacturing process. The third partner was a sales guy: he didn't care *what* he sold, if he could make money doing it.

Since each had a personal specialty, you would think they would complement the other and together they'd make a winning team. Exactly the opposite happened. Each wanted the company to be something different. Each had his own priorities. Possessing no shared vision or plan, they constantly fought over money, staff, and resources until, unable to survive in an atmosphere of constant chaos, the business collapsed.

Don't be like the "Three Cannabis Guys." Have a vision. Have a plan. Then stick to it.

## POWER HOMEWORK

Get your journal out again to ponder these questions:

1. Do you have a vision? Is it inspiring, clear, and linked to your market?

**2.** Have you explained your vision to your team? Why or why not?

**3.** Can people recite your vision? In the months before the launch of the Mac, Steve Jobs met with the team frequently. At each he reinforced the "Four Key Points of the Macintosh Launch." He quizzed people on it. Thirty-eight years later, Steve can still remember three of the four points. Will your people be able to recite your vision thirty years from now?

**4.** If you need to course-correct on your vision, can you "re-load" and make the argument for change?

*Chapter*

# RISE TO THE CHALLENGE

As a child, you may have played a game called "King of the Mountain." Its rules are about as simple as you can get: a bunch of kids scramble up an earthen mound or, in winter, a large snow pile, each trying to be the first to reach the summit. Once a "king" is established, the other kids try to knock them down and take their place. This battle for supremacy continues until everyone exhausts themselves and gives up. (We told you it was simple.)

The origins of "King of the Mountain" (or its other name, "King of the Hill") are shrouded in antiquity. But the impulsive struggle behind the need to assume and challenge dominance appears to be built into our DNA. Among our closest genetic relatives, chimpanzees and gorillas, young males regularly challenge older, established "alphas" for dominance over the community. Male moose, elk, and rams literally "lock horns" and "butt heads" every mating season to determine who among them will have first pick of prime breeding partners. Even birds fight for dominance, hence the phrase "pecking order."

Our literature is also filled with classic stories about characters who fight to gain and hold power against challengers. From Shakespeare's *Macbeth* to George Orwell's *Animal Farm* to George R. R. Martin's A Song of Ice and Fire (aka *Game of Thrones*), we are raised on tales about people who must fight challengers, from both within and without, to clutch on to and maintain power.

As the boss, you can—and should—expect to be challenged. Frequently. It's a fact of leadership. Challenges can come from many directions, sometimes simultaneously. Partners may challenge you for dominance. Managers and employees may challenge your authority, your resolve, and your decision-making abilities. Vendors may challenge your patience and your standards. Even customers may try to get the better of you or challenge you to do better.

Knowing this, you need a vision for how you will respond to such challenges when they arise. No one wants to work for someone who, when challenged, lashes out in anger or, perhaps even worse, sulks. If you can deal with your challenges in an effective way, you'll be a model for your employees.

How you deal with conflict will also determine whether you develop self-respect and the respect of others. Effective leaders don't fall apart at the first hint of conflict. They stay faithful to their vision and work to understand and overcome the conflicts they initiate or find in their way.

If you're like most people, your knee-jerk reaction to any challenge to your authority will be defensive. You will initially protect any vulnerable flanks and then, if the threat continues, fight back. But while such a primal reaction is understandable, giving in to your impulses is rarely a winning strategy. Because not all challenges are necessarily threatening. If handled properly, some can even be useful and ultimately strengthen your power position.

Step one is to determine where the challenge is coming from and the intent behind it. Not all challenges are hostile. Not every adversary is an enemy out to destroy you. Some challenges spring from genuine confusion over objectives or directions, and responding to them can clarify situations, getting everyone moving in tandem. Others can come from a genuine desire to improve things and may contain seeds of valuable solutions to vexing problems. Yet other challenges *are* indeed malignant and warrant an appropriate, albeit proportional response.

Here are some strategies to successfully resolve some likely scenarios in the perpetual contest for power:

## CHALLENGES FROM PARTNERS

If you have partners, expect them to question or even outright contest your decisions and actions, especially if your business is having problems. If sales are down, if profits haven't met expectations, if growth has slowed, or if multiple one-star reviews explode on Yelp, your partners will likely start pointing fingers, and those will be directed at *you*.

If recriminations become too frequent, it's probably because you didn't establish your power at the onset. You must make it clear from day one you are the one in charge, and you must have the latitude to act as you see fit (and then be accountable for the results).

If you don't take time to address this situation, it'll only fester and worsen. Like the story of Malcolm, so often partners come together without discussing power and then, unsurprisingly, struggle with status and authority. They're unable to decide who will do what and be responsible for discrete parts of the business. Then, because so much is at stake, everyone feels they can weigh in on everything. This FOMO, or fear of missing out, creates confusion and frustration, which slows decision-making, none of which is good for an entrepreneurial endeavor.

## CHALLENGES FROM EMPLOYEES

Monday Morning Quarterbacking is a favorite activity among employees. It's easy to have "brilliant ideas" and know what's best for the organization when you don't have to shoulder actual responsibility for the consequences.

While you can dismiss criticism and even active push-back from staff as predictable grousing, don't be too quick to reject it out of hand. Often, criticism from a manager or an employee is really a suggestion in disguise. If the challenge seems benign, follow up by challenging the critic to propose a solution. The subordinate may actually have a constructive idea you can use.

Another common challenge from employees we shall call "testing limits." It's the kind kids regularly pose to parents to see how much crap they can get away with. But instead of resisting bedtimes, using bad language, and staying out beyond curfew, these challenges can take the form of coming in late, leaving early, abusing sick days, petty theft, and general slacking off. Establish your authority by making it clear that while you understand no one is perfect, habitual flaunting of company rules will not be tolerated.

As with dealing with children, it's important to set rules. You can't expect your team to know what will be tolerated and what won't be without clear explanations. And, yes, people might think you're uncool because you're a "rule-maker," but better to take that step than to sink into a morass of organizational uncertainty, conflict, and missed expectations.

Sparky Rose, co-founder and managing partner of the Chicago-based cannabis consulting firm Supercritical, once opined to Steve that too many firms, once you peel back the veneer on their operations, are in trouble. "No one knows what's going on in most cannabis companies. It's absolute mayhem."

Like an overly permissive parent, a lenient boss will end up with a staff of spoiled brats.

Related sidenote: you are probably familiar with the story of the *HMS Bounty*, the 18th century British merchant vessel that was the site of the famous mutiny. According to popular legend, it was the tyrannical behavior of the ship's captain, William Bligh, that led to the crew's rebellion.

Yet history tells a much different story.

When the ship arrived in Tahiti in September 1788 to collect breadfruit plants to feed Britain's colonial enslaved people, Bligh relaxed military discipline to the point that when it was time to leave five months later, the crew no longer had any interest in completing their mission. Bligh tried to restore discipline, but by then it was too late.

Led by first officer Fletcher Christian, the crew threw Bligh and his few loyalists into an open boat and took off as fugitives. The lesson of the mutiny on the *Bounty*? You can relinquish power to subordinates, but don't eliminate the rules and then try to enforce them. It's nearly impossible to get power back once you've decided to abrogate it.

## CHALLENGES FROM VENDORS

Like any business, a vendor or supplier will operate in their own best interest, not yours. As a result, they are likely to slow deliveries, raise prices, deliver incomplete shipments, and otherwise cut corners whenever they have an economic incentive to do so. As with other stakeholders in your orbit, you must set expectations early, then enforce these performance standards. If a vendor finds it can fail to meet contractual obligations without consequence, it will do so. The only way to maintain your power is to exercise it. Use it or lose it.

## CHALLENGES FROM CUSTOMERS

Customers are the lifeblood of your business, so you must be circumspect in how you respond to their complaints, criticisms, and demands. Take complaints seriously as "warning signs" that you're doing something wrong, and you must improve.

The old saying, "The customer is always right," has relevance in this situation. However, you will inevitably encounter customers who are just out to abuse you, to try to get something for nothing. When their behavior crosses the line, you are within your rights, in fact, you are obligated, to "fire" that customer to retain your business's integrity and your power position within it.

. . .

We all need to get past our egos when it comes to challenges. Discerning the intentions of our opponent is necessary to understanding how you should respond. If the challenge does not affect your company's mission, then you need to check yourself. This is not about turning the other cheek. It's about staying focused on what matters.

Ultimately, you must view every challenge as a chance for improvement. For example, there was once a canna-business that put out a product with a special kind of branding their customers had come to know and love. For years, sales were strong and steady. But then, without warning, business begin to slide. No one could explain it.

One employee came up with the novel idea of "scoring" their flower products in terms of their common effects on users. They could rate each product on a scale of 1 to 10 on its ability to make you hungry, horny, sleepy, happy, etc. This approach was completely at odds with how the company had marketed its products in the past, and the CEO took the suggestion as an insult and betrayal of the brand he had worked so long and hard to establish.

The CEO's reaction was so strong the "treasonous" employee feared for her job. But cooler heads ultimately prevailed, and the CEO was persuaded to try this new approach. After some tweaks, the rebranded products were launched to great success. Sales increased, and profits soared.

Yes, there will always be people who cannot tolerate being challenged. (Sonny Corleone?) Be wiser than that. Whenever you feel triggered, it's time for a gut check: Are you acting in concert with your vision? If so, don't take it personally. Does the person challenging you have your best interest at heart? If so, engage with them to advance the needs of your company. Not your ego.

## POWER HOMEWORK

Using your journal, reflect on the following:

1. How do you react when challenged?

2. Do you seek to understand the challenge before responding? Do you want to listen to what you're being told, or attack?

3. When you're challenged, do you think it signals a lack of respect for you—or your position?

4. What can you do to calm yourself when challenged so you don't react negatively?

# Chapter

# LEADERS, BRING JOY TO YOUR WORKPLACE

Leaders need "followers." That's axiomatic. As a business owner, you'll find building your army of people, otherwise known as your *team*, will be straightforward. You will either reach out to the local community via advertising and/or the Internet, you will get referrals from friends and/or other business owners, or candidates will come directly to you looking for work. (Now that we are in the age of remote working, many employers are also finding they can also reach a non-local talent pool.)

Of course, not all candidates will be qualified. Not all will have the kind of skills or experience you demand. Others will simply not have the personalities or temperaments befitting your organization. But over time, you will find the right people to occupy the right positions and your company will be up and running.

That's the easy part.

The hard part? Keeping your staff intact and productive,

avoiding absenteeism, defections, and burnout. As we have pointed out many times, some leaders use the authoritarian approach to keep their troops in line, ruling through fear and intimidation. They set impossibly high standards, then berate employees when they predictably fail. They try to motivate staff through threats of demotion or termination. They dock pay, refuse to pay bonuses, or impose penalties for even minor performance infractions.

It doesn't take a business genius to realize "ruling with an iron fist" rarely works. In fact, it's likely to be counterproductive. People have options, and if you abuse your power and your people, it will lead to poor morale, constant staff turnover, and low productivity.

In case you haven't figured it out yet, there's a secret to keeping a mighty and motivated staff: *People like working for companies where they like to work. And they work better when they work for people who they like or at least respect.*

Put simply, when people feel happy at their jobs, they're more likely to show up and do good work than when they're miserable. When a workplace is a place of joy, and even challenge, but not terror, they're less likely to leave. Even for more money.

You can instill the happiness you seek by creating a vision of a joyful and productive workplace. Silicon Valley knows this well. Possessing one of the most competitive employee markets on the planet, it realized the value of workplace joy years ago. It has since become famous for offering employees opportunities for growth as well as all manner of perks ranging from free gourmet meals to complimentary childcare to personal shoppers to rec rooms stuffed with pinball and videogames.

There's a method to such madness. The point was to keep staff engaged and on premises as much as possible and away from poachers. And it worked. Not only has Silicon Valley maintained its crown as the world's epicenter of technological innovation, but many of its workplace practices have become models for companies in other industries worldwide.

Fortunately, you needn't have the deep pockets of Apple or Google or Facebook to produce and retain a happy staff. You just need to treat your people well and create an environment where they can grow. All of this will help you build your company and increase your power.

Some simple ways to bring joy to the workplace include:

### 1. PUT ON A HAPPY FACE.

This might seem simplistic, but you'd be amazed at how many bosses use Ebenezer Scrooge as their role model. If you show up every day with your face in a scowl, constantly complain about how tough your job is, and basically grump your way to closing time, why be surprised if you find yourself leading a staff of miserable, underperforming, and unaccountable people? A positive, upbeat workplace starts with *you*. So, greet your workers with a smile and see how contagious a good mood becomes.

### 2. PUBLICLY RECOGNIZE GOOD WORK.

More than just offering a hearty "attaboy" when someone does a good job, regularly bring your staff together to call out and praise your top performers. It's also worth acknowledging people who have worked hard—even if the outcome wasn't what you hoped for. Public recognition is far more powerful and motivating than private praise.

### 3. INTERMITTENT REWARDS.

One of the most insidious ways casinos keep gamblers glued to slot machines is via what's known as "intermittent reward." Small "wins" that show up at unpredictable intervals have an almost irresistible appeal, leading to addiction-like behavior. To entice your staff, give them small rewards, like fresh doughnuts, a catered lunch, or let them leave an hour early. But don't make all your company perks regular and predictable, or the novelty will wear off and they will become viewed as entitlements.

### 4. AVOID MICROMANAGING.

We've mentioned this before, but it bears repeating. What employees hate more than anything is being repeatedly told how to do their jobs. Give your workers as much latitude as possible, even if it means allowing them to screw up every now and then. Failure is a great teacher, and a solution they discover for themselves rather than being force-fed will be better retained. And they'll feel better about themselves and you as a result.

## 5. PROMOTE PRIDE THROUGH PURPOSE.

We have talked about how every company needs a *mission*, and how it must be embraced by each employee. At work, it's far too easy to become lost in the minutia of an immediate task, to forget why the company is in business in the first place. To maintain high morale and employee engagement, regularly show your employees how their work is contributing to the company's success, and how that success is impacting the community at large. When employees believe they are *doing good*, that they are *changing the world*, they will approach their work with pride and enthusiasm.

## 6. FOSTER A HEALTHY WORK-LIFE BALANCE.

One of the leading causes of burnout is an over-emphasis on work. We hear much about the value of the "American work ethic" and reward people who toil for long hours. In fact, at many companies, overtime is a way of life. But multiple studies have shown workaholics are notoriously unproductive. In fact, most people are only productive for about four or five hours a day. It's just the way we're built. To create a happy workplace, encourage your staff to take their earned time off, spend moments with family, and pursue personal interests and hobbies. Oh, and that goes for the boss too!

. . .

Yes, there will be times when you must push forward, when you must push your people to the limit. But there is wisdom to letting people breathe. More importantly, getting this right can lead to more power for you. Do not get so caught up in winning and working you don't celebrate the joys in life.

Instead, leadership should roughly parallel the relationship one has with a child. The leader gets the joy of lessons learned, of seeing their people and themselves stretched. Of course, parenting isn't easy. It can be downright exhausting. But there is nothing more rewarding than seeing someone for whom you are responsible succeed.

To this end, Steve once worked with a client; we'll call him Will. Will was considered a great leader and had grown his organization from scratch. When Steve met him, 60 people worked for him, but he had to make all the decisions himself. Over time, Steve helped Will realize he must share responsibility, not just for his own mental health, but to build pride and increased accountability in his employees.

So, on Steve's advice, Will tried to delegate. Oddly, his subordinates resisted. They had gotten so used to Will overseeing everything they were afraid to make decisions for themselves. Turns out, Will had infantilized most of his staff. Now he was reaping what he had sown.

Fast forward three months. Steve had lunch with Will. He said he had been having issues with his CFO, named Catherine. The two had been constantly butting heads over one issue or another. Initially, Will had reverted to his old ways, becoming an authoritarian, demanding things be done his way.

But then he had had an epiphany. He realized Catherine had found the courage to stand up to him. She was not only able to formulate strong arguments for her positions but also lay them out in a manner both powerful and convincing.

Rather than be offended his CFO was challenging his power, Will felt a rush of pride. Here was a person he had previously doubted, yet whom he had empowered with decision-making authority, and now she was making the most of it! This made for a joyful situation, as power was being expanded even as it was being shared.

In classic fairy tales like *Sleeping Beauty* to such modern fables as Disney's *The Lion King* and George Lucas's original Star Wars trilogy, kingdoms fall into depression and disrepair when the crown is seized by ruthless authoritarians, only to experience joyous renewal when just rulers are returned to power, and "peace and freedom" are restored to the land.

Rule your kingdom with a velvet glove, strive to make it the happiest place on earth, and all can indeed live happily ever after.

## POWER HOMEWORK

Use your journal to answer the following:

1. Do you think joy has a place in your workplace, or is work not an environment for inspiring joy?

**2.** What do you do to create joy in your work-place?

**3.** Have you worked in places that were joyful? What did you love most about this job?

**4.** How many of the attributes of your joyful workplace have you replicated in your current company?

**5.** Is leadership, at least some of the time, joyful for you or a drudge? If it's a struggle, ask yourself why and whether you want to continue in this manner.

*Chapter*

# YES, YOU ARE HERE TO CHANGE THE WORLD

Today, virtually every company, regardless of size, is expected to write a "mission statement." What is a "mission statement"? The website Investopedia.com explains it this way: "A mission statement is used by a company to explain, in simple and concise terms, its purpose(s) for being. The statement is generally short, either a single sentence or a short paragraph."

Shopify.com has a somewhat more detailed definition: "A mission statement is a brief description of why a company or nonprofit organization exists. In one to three sentences, it explains what the company does, who it serves, and what differentiates it from competitors. It's used to provide focus, direction, and inspiration to employees while it tells customers or clients what to expect from the business."

Now, if you're cynical, you might say <u>all</u> companies exist for the same purpose: *To make money.* But if that's what you think, you're missing the point. There are hundreds, hell, *thousands* of ways to "make money." If "making money" was all business was about, we'd all be investment bankers.

Okay, fine. Companies make money, but they do so by *filling a need in people's lives.* And the best companies approach their mission with an almost religious-like fervor. In the best of cases, this zeal breeds a cult-like devotion among customers, a degree of loyalty allowing companies to prosper in both good times and bad.

You no doubt know of people whose allegiance to some companies rivals the fidelity sports fans have to their favorite teams. We're talking about those who worship at the altar of Apple, Ferrari, Coca-Cola, In-N-Out Burger, Trader Joe's, Disney, Marvel, Ikea, Starbucks, Zappos, or Harley-Davidson. Such customers virtually drool in anticipation of new product announcements, can recite company origin stories like chapters from the Old Testament, and consider defections to a competing brand as heresy.

Consider Apple, Steve's alma mater. Fellow Steves— Jobs and Wozniak—founded this consumer electronics and e-services juggernaut in the mid-1970s. But Apple didn't become one of the world's highest-valued companies because Jobs told his folks to make products cheaper so others would buy them.

That's limited, purely transactional thinking. No, when preparing to release the revolutionary Macintosh in 1984, Jobs famously said, "We're here to put a dent in the universe. Otherwise, why even be here?" His goal was to literally change the world. (And we can say that, in no small way, he succeeded.)

Jobs laid his own vision down in this mission statement, penned in 1977: "Apple is dedicated to the empowerment of man—to making personal computing accessible to each and every individual so as to help change the way we think, work, learn, and communicate." That's pretty heady thinking for two tofu-munching, sandal-wearing geeks working out of a garage in Cupertino.

Just to make sure you get the idea, here are a few mission statements from companies you may also recognize:

- **THE COCA-COLA COMPANY**
  "To refresh the world, to inspire moments of optimism and happiness, to create value and make a difference."

- **THE WALT DISNEY COMPANY**
  "To entertain, inform and inspire people around the globe through the power of unparalleled storytelling, reflecting the iconic brands, creative minds and innovative technologies that make ours the world's premier entertainment company."

- **NIKE**
  "To expand human potential by creating groundbreaking sport innovations, by making our products more sustainably, by building a creative and diverse global team and by making a positive impact in communities where we live and work."

- **SPOTIFY**
  "Our mission is to unlock the potential of human creativity—by giving a million creative

artists the opportunity to live off their art and billions of fans the opportunity to enjoy and be inspired by it."

● **TESLA**
"To accelerate the world's transition to sustainable energy."

Now, notice nowhere in any of these mission statements does it say, "to make money." Everyone wants to be part of something that matters. They want to believe their life has meaning and purpose. People who go into medicine, the arts, or the priesthood often talk about responding to a "calling," that the universe compels them to follow their career path.

Similarly, people who devote their lives to the armed forces, teaching, or firefighting often say they do so out of a sense of "duty." Again, they are serving a cause greater than their own limited self-interest. Certainly, people who join the Peace Corps become environmental activists, practice pro bono law, or become teachers of any sort aren't just in it for the money.

When it comes to accumulating power, powerful leaders have always had the ability to instill a sense of "greater purpose" in their followers, whether it was George Washington rallying the troops at Valley Forge in the cause of national independence, Maximilien de Robespierre calling upon the people of Paris to fight for "liberty, equality, fraternity," or Steve Jobs asking his employees to "make a dent in the universe."

Of course, if you can combine passion with profit, so much the better. Great companies manage to do both. And so must yours if it's ever going to be great. Unfortunately, too many cannabusiness owners lose sight of "the dream," replacing the aspirational with the functional. Sure, it might seem more "practical" to focus on the day-to-day details, but at what cost?

(By the way, if we had a dollar for every time a cannabusiness leader told us they couldn't create a mission statement because "the market is moving too fast," well, we wouldn't need to write this book!) But back to leadership, if your people aren't excited about coming to work—if they don't feel like their efforts are setting the world on fire—you're missing a huge component of acquiring and maintaining power.

Yes, your business may sputter along like a 15-year-old Ford Focus, merely getting you from here to there, but you will never experience the joys of true success. Companies attract and retain top talent by being visionaries. They also entice customers by communicating a sense of being "more than."

This means if you want to differentiate yourself, if you want to motivate your people to deliver the best they have to offer, you must "Think Different" (as Apple so memorably posited in 1997), and you must also think *bigger*. Don't settle for working on a small goal. Have a big vision. Yes, earlier in this book we mentioned the old axiom, "man makes plans and God laughs," but without a plan, without a vision, you'll be thinking small and be swept away by those who have a vision.

You can also think of your business as a crusade. A holy war. A jihad. A movement toward greatness. A revolution that can alter humankind forever. Sure, it's grandiose.

Pretentious. Bombastic. Perhaps even bordering on mega-lomaniacal. But that's the way great leaders *think*.

Then engage your team to think the way you do. It's no fun being alone on a mission. Enlist your team on this great adventure. Cannabis is expanding, changing, diversifying, and quickly evolving. It's like the internet in the late 1990s. Who knows how the industry will shake out? Who knows who will be the "winners" and who will be the "losers"? All we know is that this plant has the potential to help, amuse, and empower people.

Isn't it great to in some way be tied into that mission?

So, forget about being ordinary or pragmatic when it comes to your vision. It's always possible—and neces-sary—to articulate a higher goal. Possessing big, lofty as-pirations will move your people.

Let's illustrate this point with a personal story you may recall from our book's foreword. Tracy Ryan's child had cancer. She got into cannabis after researching ways to al-leviate her child's nausea following chemotherapy. Driven by the dream of helping not only her child, but so many others like her, Ryan spearheaded a nonprofit called Can-naKids to help other cancer sufferers—so fellow parents and their children would never have to experience the same heartache. This led to the establishment of her venture-funded company NKore, an immunotherapy and cancer research company focusing on the use of cannabinoids to attack cancer.

Before taking this plunge, Tracy had a choice: to go big or small. Digging deep within, she found untapped power in herself to change her life, better her child's circumstances, and ultimately transform the world. Like Tracy, when you have a powerful vision, you can create what Steve Jobs called a "reality distortion field." You can use power to bend reality to your will. But possessing a big, audacious goal doesn't just inspire. It brings individuals together, giving *you* power. Conversely, the smaller and more limited your view, the fewer people you will attract. The less power you will possess.

Life is not without problems. Tracy's child's medical condition was heartbreaking. Yet she rose above it by having a vision and the passion to make her solution come true. Why not use your own vision to attract the people, the funding, the insights, the supporters, and the allies to make it work?

This is no time to be humble. Nobody votes for a candidate who equivocates. And don't give in to fear, either. Don't be afraid others will laugh at you or think you're nuts. There isn't a successful inventor, entrepreneur, or artist who wasn't criticized or rejected at some point in their career. Don't listen to the haters. This world was built on big ideas, and people are seeking dreamers with grand plans. Do what you think is right to advance your power and move your company forward.

One more thing: at the close of the 1992 Academy Award–winning film *Scent of a Woman*, Al Pacino, playing retired Army lieutenant colonel Frank Slade, expresses his disappointment with life. In a mournful soliloquy he says, "Now I have come to the crossroads in my life. I always knew what the right path was. Without exception, I knew. But I never took it. You know why? It was too damn hard."

Life *is* hard. Not feeling you have the power *or* not using your power to change even a small portion of the world makes for a disappointing life.

Don't make Slade's mistake. Use your power. And look. Even if reality turns out to be only a fraction of your fantasy, as least you'll have moved in the right direction. As the saying goes, "Reach for the stars, and you'll never end up with a handful of mud."

# AFTERWORD

Beneath the rushing, hustling, bustling, frenetic energy of modern life, a disquieting question lurks. Unbidden, undesired, it haunts us with its insistence. In our quiet moments, it especially gnaws at us, threatening to destroy everything we love, all we hold dear.

The question is this: *Just how long will this last?*

Like life, power is not eternal. Tomorrow is not a given. Neither is power. We never know when either will be taken from us, making them so precious.

As children, we don't think in these terms. Blissfully cocooned in the wonder of playing, our imaginations afire with make-believe, we can scarcely believe in bedtimes, let alone anything as final as death.

Yet, as adults, we cannot help but recognize the impermanence of it all—how fleeting the good and the bad moments really are. The wisest among us come to realize a heart-wrenching yet freeing truth: this, too, shall pass. Likewise, the savviest among us know power ebbs and flows and we are merely its custodians for a time, *not* its source.

Returning to kids, we find another useful analogy in Kahlil Gibran's famous book, *The Prophet*:

Your children are not your children.
They are the sons and daughters of Life's
    longing for itself.
They come through you but not from you,
And though they are with you, yet they belong
    not to you.

You may give them your love but not your
    thoughts,
For they have their own thoughts.
You may house their bodies but not their souls,
For their souls dwell in the house of tomorrow,
    which you cannot visit, not even in your
    dreams . . .

Just as our kids are not truly ours, so, too, are we custodians of power—and not its owners. As parents we may enable our offspring to experience wonderful lives, bringing good to the world.

But we can just as easily founder in our caretaking responsibilities. Through our efforts—or the lack thereof—our children can mess up, sometimes in terrible ways. The difference in outcomes can often come down to how engaged we are in this process and how well we live up to our duties. Or not.

History supplies too many instances of this dereliction. All kinds of despots and tyrants have used their time with power for horrific ends, committing unspeakable acts, doing irreparable harm. As parent of your own company, be sure to act as its steward, informed by integrity, the same way you would guide your kids.

Now that you have learned the *Power Up* principles, our message to you is simple yet crucial: use the limited time you possess power for good. Not just for yourself but others. Central to our ideas in this book has been the issue of trust. We stressed its two-way nature: urging you to realize your team will be likelier to follow you as their leader—so long as you earn and maintain trust.

Recognizing the fickleness of power, understanding that our days are numbered, we implore you to use this limited yet vital resource in humanity's service. For the time being, you are a player in the most magnificent of plays, the pageantry of existence. While upon its stage, should you take care to do well by your people and the world at large, perhaps we can not only escape the historical nightmares that have plagued humanity for so long, but create something more resembling a heaven on earth.

At least that's our hope, our vision of what's possible. (Throughout these pages we have asked you to dream bigger; now we are following our own advice.)

Of course, it's easy to feel discouraged by life's impermanence. You have every right to be dismayed by the reality that all we create is little more than castles in the sand. But that's not the full story. Like life, your power is not infinite. It will come to an end. Use it now.

You are more powerful than you think.

As we come to a close, we encourage you to appreciate the responsibility and privilege afforded in your role. You are given an incredible gift to bring untold wonders to this world through your actions and words. Know your days are numbered, but also recognize what a true honor it is to live them well—to live powerfully.

# ABOUT THE AUTHORS

## *Steve Scheier*

Steve Scheier is a leadership culti-
vator, author, and speaker serving
high profile clients in the cannabis
and hemp industries since 2018.
Utilizing his Cannabis CoreTM
program, Steve works with cannabis and hemp innova-
tors to enhance how they think about and use power, focus
their vision, increase their leadership, and improve their
decision-making.

Steve's background in politics, marketing, organizational development, and educational policy has enabled
him to create dynamic teachings that empower leaders and
their organizations.

From 2011–18, he worked as a consultant in the nonprofit sector, where he focused on improving organizational decision-making. He is the author of the 2015 book
*Do More Good. Better: Using the Power of Decision Clarity to
Mobilize the Talent of Your Nonprofit Team.*

Prior to his consulting career, Steve served as the vice
president of human resources at a nonprofit and at two
technology companies.

Before his efforts in the human resources field, Steve
worked at Apple in several marketing and program leadership positions. Steve worked closely with Steve Jobs from

1982–1985 and through that experience learned a great deal about how to articulate a vision, strengthen leaders, and mobilize teams.

As a member of nearly a dozen executive teams, Steve has supported and reported to CEOs for more than 30 years.

Steve has a B.A. in Russian History and an M.A. in Education Policy from University of California, Berkeley, plus significant coursework in organizational development at the University of San Francisco.

### Michael Ashley

Michael began his writing career as a newspaper reporter and playwright before transitioning to Hollywood to work for the head of the literary department at Creative Artists Agency. He served as a screenwriter for Disney in which he sold the treatment for the hit Halloween movie *Girl vs Monster*. A former professor, Michael has written over 30 books on many subjects. He recently co-authored *Own the A.I. Revolution* (McGraw Hill) which launched at the United Nations and was named by Soundview as one of 2019's top business books. Michael serves as a columnist for *Forbes*, *Entrepreneur*, and *Green Entrepreneur*.

Beyond running his own creative content agency, Michael is the author of four bestsellers. His writing has been featured in *Entertainment Weekly*, *The National Examiner*, the United Nations' *ITU News*, *The Orange County Business*

*Journal*, and *The Orange County Register*. Michael special-
izes in turning his clients into thought leaders via ghost-
writing and consulting with businesses on storytelling,
messaging, and branding.

Author photos by (*Steve Scheier*) Sarah Tyack and
(*Michael Ashley*) Remi + Tori Photography

Made in the USA
Middletown, DE
23 October 2021